SELLING SOLUTIONS

REDEFINING VALUE
INSTEAD OF
NEGOTIATING PRICE

TUCKER W. "BILL" MAIN, FCSI, FMP

This publication is intended to provide accurate and authoritative information in regard to the subject matter covered. It is sold with the understanding that the publisher is not engaged in rendering legal, accounting or other professional services. If legal advice or other expert assistance is required, the services of a competent professional person should be sought.

ISBN 1-891356-03-8

ATTENTION ASSOCIATIONS AND MULTI-UNIT OPERATORS:
Quantity discounts are available on bulk purchases of this book for premiums, sales promotions, or educational purposes. Custom imprinting can also be done to fit specific needs. Please contact: Bill Main & Associates, 2220 St. George Ln., Chico, CA 95926 (800) 858-7876, e-mail: billmain@aol.com, Fax: (530)345-0212

This book is dedicated to my parents, Tim and Margaret Main, who live in retirement on a small ranch in Loma Rica, California. Without their total support and belief in me—through the trials and tribulations, heartbreaks and failures, challenges and opportunities of my career—this book would never have been possible.

Thanks, folks.

TWM

Table of Contents

Introduction

I hope Selling Solutions will enable you to take a strong, well-placed next step in charting a successful career. The message is clear: You must take a strategic approach to selling through developing a consulting relationship with your customers. Whether your customers are single-unit independents, high-profile chains, or non-commercial operators, integrating these guiding principles into your sales regimen will give you a distinct competitive edge and add value to the products you sell.

Added value means less negotiation about price and a renewed focus on the inherent profit potential your products offer. More importantly, your customers will develop a greater respect for you. No longer will you be simply an order taker, interested only in selling food, supplies and equipment. You will be a consultant, offering ideas, information, and tangible solutions to provide an immediate and measurable profit boost to your customer's business. This is the first step in developing win-win relationships.

Thinking like a consultant is probably not much different from the way you think about selling right now. Consultative selling, however, requires systematizing and formalizing the sales process into actionable steps. The goal is simple: Establish credibility with your customers. This will boost their confidence in you, and move them to greater appreciation for the company you represent.

Your new role as consultant will also foster a feeling of dependence and a sense of loyalty. When your customer thinks about purchasing food or supplies, your name will come to mind. This top-of-mind awareness is the foundation for building long-term relationships, and is a precious commodity when dealing with foodservice owners and managers in all segments of the industry.

Today's competition can be fierce. Often, you share accounts with other suppliers and distributors. Your credibility as a consultative salesperson and competence in meeting your customer's needs will immediately help differentiate you from your competition. Once you have achieved your competitive edge, it will be critical to constantly reinforce your value. Should you fail to do this, you will remain forever in bondage to the question: "What have you done for me lately?" Does that sound familiar?

Selling Solutions was written as a companion guide to my live presentation on the subject of consultative selling in foodservice distribution. It is intended to help you make the transition from being a salesperson to being a consultant. With this simple, results-producing tool in hand, you can call on your next customer with new confidence and a real competitive advantage.

Welcome to the world of consultative selling—where you don't just sell products, you sell solutions.

PART ONE

THE NEW DIRECTION

CHAPTER 1

WHY SHOULD WE CARE?

THE PARABLE OF "THE MAGIC NICKEL"

"How can I sell my customers on value instead of price?" This is the question distributors ask me more frequently than any other. So I asked myself if I could reshape the DSR selling discipline to encompass the following elements: meaningful product expertise, identification of food-merchandising opportunities and proven techniques to solve menu challenges.

How can a DSR take the high ground in the competitive battle being waged in foodservice distribution and still get the order? Instead of developing a plan, most DSR's continue to bicker and argue with their customers about price, price, price! If this is what's happening to you, I'd like to show you a way to break away from this non-productive pattern by trying something new.

To help foster a more positive, productive and profitable working relationship between foodservice operators and the distribution community, I have put on my "operator's hat." I hope to offer a fresh perspective; one that reveals why operators—commercial and non-commercial, independent and chain—are so stubbornly and passionately focused on price. I hope this "reality check" will help you better understand your customers, and develop better sales strategies and tactical programs to help you get the order.

Here's the reality of foodservice today: First, competition for the discretionary foodservice dollar gets fiercer every year. Convenience stores, grocery stores, home delivery, and home meal replacement have all entered into the foodservice market. Corporate foodservice continues to grow, with such mega-companies as McDonald's, Marriott, and Burger King increasing market share at a dizzying pace. The defining line between market segments continues to blur; for instance, fine dining operations are offering delivery, and many quick service outlets are drive-thru or take-out only. In addition, mid-scale casual operations are multiplying in both commercial and non-commercial venues.

Second, today's consumer is a discriminating buyer, with a more educated palate. They're much more likely to notice and appreciate quality, or the lack of it. Television can claim some credit for the increased awareness and discrimination, but more importantly, there are ten times more culinary arts programs in the United States today than ten years ago. The American Culinary Federation has become a powerful force, and has a tremendous influence on the art and science of food production and delivery. Culinary arts programs have raised the standards for the manufacturer, the operator, and the guest.

Third, government regulatory compliance continues to be the operator's worst nightmare. Whether it's I-9's or tip reporting, smoking or safety guidelines, government influence at all levels increases every year. Operators spend a larger percentage of their time fighting government instead of taking care of their guests and properly managing their employees. Operators aren't spending their time on the things that make them money.

Lastly, the average operator has a paper-thin profit margin compared to other businesses—a mere nickel on every dollar of sales. And that's if they do everything right! Coupled with an awesome workload of 70–80 hours per week, it's no wonder that the operator usually thinks small. Instead of concentrating on the "big picture" that shows value as the key ingredient to long-term success, the operator's focus is on getting lower prices from the distributor. Far too many operators chase the quick- fix, short term path and leave the value-based long term path to chance.

There are some independents and chains that make considerably more than a nickel in profit for every dollar in sales. But for the vast majority of foodservice operators across the full range of market segments, the "magic nickel" is all that can be conjured up.

Where does all the profit go? To better understand the operator mentality, let's follow the average dollar in revenue as it moves downward through the various expense categories. My purpose is to illustrate the key categories that have the most impact on your customer's profitability. If you understand the pricing and purchasing decisions of your customers, you can develop a better appreciation for their focus on price and their relative indifference to value.

It's important to use the Uniform System of Accounts for Restaurants as the standard reporting format when analyzing the impact of costs on profits. The "Uniform System" establishes a standardized listing of expenses, and details a precise order for reporting them on the Income Statement. This allows an "apples-to-apples" comparison between foodservice operations.

Figure 1 shows the total food and beverage sales that have been generated over a four-week period. Cost of Sales (Figure 2), a combination of food and beverage costs, is determined by taking a complete physical inventory of all consumable food and beverage products at the beginning of

FIGURE 1

TOTAL COSTS PER SALES DOLLAR: 95¢

Sales	
Food Sales	75¢
Beverage Sales	25¢
Total Sales	$1.00

Cost of Sales	
Food Cost (35% of Food Sales)	27¢
Beverage Cost (25% of Beverage Sales)	6¢
Total Cost of Sales	33¢

Gross Profit	67¢

Controllable Expenses	
Direct Labor	30¢
Employee Benefits	6¢
Direct Operating Expenses	5¢
Music and Entertainment	1¢
Marketing	2¢
Utility Services	3¢
General and Administrative	4¢
Repairs and Maintenance	2¢
Total Controllable Expenses	53¢

Income Before Occupancy Costs	14¢

Occupancy Costs	
Rent/Lease Expense	7¢
Property Taxes & Insurance	2¢
Total Occupancy Costs	9¢

Income Before Interest and Depreciation	5¢

the period, then adding the purchases for that same period of time. This is the total of all goods available for sale. Deduct from this number the inventory left at the end of the period, and you have the cost of goods sold. Simply put: beginning inventory + purchases – ending inventory = cost of goods sold. Cost of goods sold is also referred to as Cost of Sales.

Food and beverage cost ratios are figured differently than all other expense categories. To calculate the food cost ratio, divide food cost of goods sold by food sales. Beverage cost is calculated by dividing beverage cost of goods sold by beverage sales. For all other categories, the expense is divided by total sales. This is because individual cost control disciplines in food and beverage departments are much different than other categories, and they need to be monitored separately.

The day-to-day management practices and protocols associated with beverage cost control deserve individual attention in terms of storage, requisitioning, inventory techniques, purchasing, receiving, and the setting of operating "pars." Because beverages rarely spoil, relatively loose handling standards are common. The key to controlling costs in this category, therefore, is security.

By contrast, food cost controls are a reflection of effective product purchasing, handling, storage, preparation, and delivery. The shelf life of more than 60% of food products—including produce, seafood, poultry, meat, and vegetables—is as little as one or two days. The key to food cost control is awareness and day-to-day accountability.

Another important aspect of restaurant costs and profits is the food–beverage "mix." Food is usually the predominant seller, representing 70% to 80% of total sales. Beverage sales, on the other hand, represent only 20% to 30%. The higher the percentage of food sales, the greater the degree to which the operation is dependent upon food sales to generate profitability.

Beverage sales have a higher profit margin. In the past, it was assumed that an operator's main profits came from selling beverages. The best idea, then, was to offer food as an incentive to sell beverages. Generally speaking, a food cost of 35% and a beverage cost of 25% would yield a cost of sales of 28%. Therefore, the profitable ideal during the 1970s and '80s was to maintain a food–beverage "mix" of 70–30.

Responsible alcohol consumption, MADD, and health-oriented programs have contributed to a reduction in alcoholic beverage sales. The result has been a gradual shift in foodservice sales from alcohol toward food, and an 80–20 food–beverage "mix." Cost of sales has also shifted, upward from a low of 27–28% in the mid-1980s to 32–34% today (see Figure 2). And it's still rising.

The next item on the income and expense statement is Direct Labor (Figure 3), which is approximately 30% of sales. Direct labor cost includes employee and management salaries and wages, but not benefits. Employee benefits are not included because they go up in nearly direct proportion to increases in salaries and wages, rather than increases in revenues. On average, employee benefits are 20–25% of direct labor. As a result, employee benefits are not considered truly controllable expenses. When we consider direct labor cost and employee benefits, the result is a total labor expense of 36% on average. This means that 36¢ of every dollar goes to employee expenses. This reality truly reflects the labor-intensiveness of the foodservice business.

The sum of food and beverage cost of sales and direct labor cost is called prime cost (Figure 4). Nearly 63¢ of every dollar generated goes to pay raw product costs and the salaries and wages of management and employees.

FIGURE 2

FOOD AND BEVERAGE COSTS: 33% OF SALES

Sales	
Food Sales	75¢
Beverage Sales	25¢
Total Sales	$1.00

Cost of Sales	
Food Cost (35% of Food Sales)	27¢
Beverage Cost (25% of Beverage Sales)	6¢
Total Cost of Sales	33¢

Gross Profit	67¢

Controllable Expenses	
Direct Labor	30¢
Employee Benefits	6¢
Direct Operating Expenses	5¢
Music and Entertainment	1¢
Marketing	2¢
Utility Services	3¢
General and Administrative	4¢
Repairs and Maintenance	2¢
Total Controllable Expenses	53¢

Income Before Occupancy Costs	14¢

Occupancy Costs	
Rent/Lease Expense	7¢
Property Taxes & Insurance	2¢
Total Occupancy Costs	9¢

Income Before Interest and Depreciation	5¢

Prime cost is a measurement of cost-control performance. Food, beverage and labor costs are the key controllable expenses. Management's ability and desire to control costs and produce profits are measured by how well prime cost is controlled.

The next expense category in the "Uniform System" reporting process is "other controllable expenses" (Figure 5). This category includes Employee Benefits, Direct Operating Expenses, Music and Entertainment, Marketing, Energy, Administrative and General, and Repairs and Maintenance. In our example, other controllable expenses represent 23% of total sales. Each of the individual expense categories has numerous sub-parts, which are itemized according to the reporting requirements of the Uniform System of Accounts for Restaurants.

Figure 6 illustrates Income Before Occupancy Costs, or "operating income," as it is usually described. In the financial community, operating income is the profit generated after all controllable expenses are paid, but before allocations are made for occupancy costs. This is an important benchmark, because it is a reflection of the overall health of the foodservice concept, as well as a report card for unit management. Operating income is total controllable expenses deducted from gross profit. Making this calculation is simple and easy to understand, and the 14% operating income shown in this example is representative for the industry. To many, it is surprising to discover that only 14% of the business' revenue remains, and the rent or the mortgage has yet to be paid.

Occupancy Costs are next (Figure 7). They usually include all the typical line-item expenses associated with the "brick and mortar" of a restaurant's physical plant. Rent or mortgage payments, real estate taxes, fire and casualty insurance, personal property taxes, etc., should not exceed 10% of sales. Occupancy costs are relatively high, due to the

FIGURE 3

LABOR COSTS: 30% OF SALES

Sales	
Food Sales	75¢
Beverage Sales	25¢
Total Sales	$1.00

Cost of Sales	
Food Cost (35% of Food Sales)	27¢
Beverage Cost (25% of Beverage Sales)	6¢
Total Cost of Sales	33¢

Gross Profit	67¢

Controllable Expenses

Direct Labor	30¢

Employee Benefits	6¢
Direct Operating Expenses	5¢
Music and Entertainment	1¢
Marketing	2¢
Utility Services	3¢
General and Administrative	4¢
Repairs and Maintenance	2¢
Total Controllable Expenses	53¢

Income Before Occupancy Costs	14¢

Occupancy Costs	
Rent/Lease Expense	7¢
Property Taxes & Insurance	2¢
Total Occupancy Costs	9¢

Income Before Interest and Depreciation	5¢

cost of real estate and investments in the infrastructure. Safety and quality guidelines for such factors as air quality, grease pollution, and a multitude of other issues, add to the expenses your customers must handle.

The final result of all this activity is one nickel. Just 5¢ in profit on every dollar of sales, assuming savvy and professional management (Figure 8). To achieve this modest profit, everything must work correctly, including operating systems and cost-control measures. There must be excellent customer service standards, a loyal customer base, and lots of word-of-mouth advertising to bring in business. In short, an operator needs everything working successfully to make a nickel on a dollar.

This tiny profit is the reason the average operator is so focused on price, and often blind to value-added thinking. It's because operators don't make nearly the money they deserve for all the work that's involved. Foodservice operators are in one of the toughest businesses going. So you must be persistent, but patient with them. This should become integral to your approach to sales.

FIGURE 4

PRIME COSTS: 63% OF SALES

Sales
    Food and Beverage Sales $1.00

Prime Costs
    Food and Beverage Costs   33¢
    Direct Labor   30¢
        Total Prime Costs   63¢

Income After Prime Costs   37¢

Other Controllable Expenses
    Employee Benefits   6¢
    Direct Operating Expenses   5¢
    Music and Entertainment   1¢
    Marketing   2¢
    Utility Services   3¢
    General and Administrative   4¢
    Repairs and Maintenance   2¢
        Total Other Controllable Expenses   23¢

Income Before Occupancy Costs   14¢

Occupancy Costs
    Rent/Lease Expense   7¢
    Property Taxes & Insurance   2¢
        Total Occupancy Costs   9¢

Income Before Interest and Depreciation   5¢

FIGURE 5

OTHER CONTROLLABLE COSTS: 23%

Sales
    Food and Beverage Sales $1.00

Prime Costs
    Food and Beverage Costs   33¢
    Direct Labor   30¢
        Total Prime Costs   63¢

Income After Prime Costs   37¢

Other Controllable Expenses
    Employee Benefits   6¢
    Direct Operating Expenses   5¢
    Music and Entertainment   1¢
    Marketing   2¢
    Utility Services   3¢
    General and Administrative   4¢
    Repairs and Maintenance   2¢
        Total Other Controllable Expenses   23¢

Income Before Occupancy Costs   14¢

Occupancy Costs
    Rent/Lease Expense   7¢
    Property Taxes & Insurance   2¢
        Total Occupancy Costs   9¢

Income Before Interest and Depreciation   5¢

FIGURE 6

INCOME BEFORE OCCUPANCY COSTS: 14%

Sales
    Food and Beverage Sales $1.00

Prime Costs
    Food and Beverage Costs   33¢
    Direct Labor   30¢
        Total Prime Costs   63¢

Income After Prime Costs   37¢

Other Controllable Expenses
    Employee Benefits   6¢
    Direct Operating Expenses   5¢
    Music and Entertainment   1¢
    Marketing   2¢
    Utility Services   3¢
    General and Administrative   4¢
    Repairs and Maintenance   2¢
        Total Other Controllable Expenses   23¢

Income Before Occupancy Costs   14¢

Occupancy Costs
    Rent/Lease Expense   7¢
    Property Taxes & Insurance   2¢
        Total Occupancy Costs   9¢

Income Before Interest and Depreciation   5¢

FIGURE 7

RENT AND TAXES: 9%

Sales	
Food and Beverage Sales	$1.00
Prime Costs	
Food and Beverage Costs	33¢
Direct Labor	30¢
Total Prime Costs	63¢
Income After Prime Costs	37¢
Other Controllable Expenses	
Employee Benefits	6¢
Direct Operating Expenses	5¢
Music and Entertainment	1¢
Marketing	2¢
Utility Services	3¢
General and Administrative	4¢
Repairs and Maintenance	2¢
Total Other Controllable Expenses	23¢
Income Before Occupancy Costs	14¢
Occupancy Costs	
Rent/Lease Expense	7¢
Property Taxes & Insurance	2¢
Total Occupancy Costs	9¢
Income Before Interest and Depreciation	5¢

FIGURE 8

...AND 5% IS LEFT

Sales
    Food and Beverage Sales $1.00

Prime Costs
    Food and Beverage Costs   33¢
    Direct Labor   30¢
        Total Prime Costs   63¢

Income After Prime Costs   37¢

Other Controllable Expenses
    Employee Benefits   6¢
    Direct Operating Expenses   5¢
    Music and Entertainment   1¢
    Marketing   2¢
    Utility Services   3¢
    General and Administrative   4¢
    Repairs and Maintenance   2¢
        Total Other Controllable Expenses   23¢

Income Before Occupancy Costs   14¢

Occupancy Costs
    Rent/Lease Expense   7¢
    Property Taxes & Insurance   2¢
        Total Occupancy Costs   9¢

Income Before Interest and Depreciation   5¢

CHAPTER 2

THINKING LIKE
A CONSULTANT

The traditional role of the distributor sales representative has been that of an ordertaker. Today, ordering can be done automatically via fax, voice mail and on-line ordering systems. The order-taking function of the DSR will not be as significant in the distribution business in the year 2000 as it is today. The future lies with DSR's who can proactively provide customized product solutions to a wide variety of problems: food cost control, menu engineering, internal merchandising techniques, sourcing new supplies, and equipment specifications. Therefore, it is time to begin the transition from order taker to consultant. Are you ready for the transition?

Consultants are expected to be experts on every facet of a client's business—from food products to workers' compensation, from processing credit cards to fixing a dishwashing machine. But the good news is that foodservice and hospitality consultants can have "niche" specialties. There are food and recipe development chefs, mystery shopping services, operating-systems and cost-control experts, employee trainers, and many more. As a DSR, your extensive product knowledge already qualifies you as an industry expert, and your years of experience in the field have given you the opportunity to observe and learn from your customers. As Yogi Berra says, "You can observe a lot by just watching."

In the highly competitive foodservice distribution community, sales reps are generally viewed by street, chain, and non-commercial operators as problem-solvers. They have come to rely on the quality and price/value of the products you provide. But now, a whole new era is unfolding in which your customers will view you in a new light—as a consultant. You will have to rely more and more on your imagination, technical skills, knowledge, and personal integrity. You will be asked to provide additional value, new services, and business operations expertise as part of the relationship-building process.

The first step in adjusting to your new role as a consultant is conducting a needs assessment for all of your existing and prospective customers. Whether you seek greater account penetration, or you are trying to re-energize your "cold-call" regimen, a needs assessment will give you a profile of who your customers are, what drives their purchasing decisions, how their menus are configured, and what logical points of access exist for you to begin making an immediate impact on their profitability. I'll walk you through the needs assessment in Chapter 4.

The most challenging aspect of the shift from salesperson to profitability consultant is working within a new mind-set—one that reprioritizes how you think about the sales and profits of your customers in relation to the other considerations of your business. Your customers' sales-building activities and their overall profit performance must be placed above your own selling quotas. As a consultant, your business is to sell solutions, not products. Your goal is to help your customers drive their sales and profits higher—to help them make more take-home cash.

This is your mission. Don't focus on making money for

yourself. When your customers begin to make money, your sales and gross profits will also begin to increase. You have a new "distributor/ operator mission statement for the year 2000" that aligns your interests with those of your customers. This mission statement reads:

> "To develop account activity that maximizes revenues and gross-profit margins to you and to the distributor, while offering value-added benefits to the operator, resulting in higher sales and profits."

The objective is to create a "win-win" situation that requires neither the distributor nor the operator to compromise on price. The margins are sufficient, and your customers, whether mid-scale café or corporate cafeteria, feel they are receiving sufficient value for the price they are paying. They will have a new sense of what value-added service really is when they review your relationship with them. Your consulting orientation will produce new and exciting opportunities for increased profits because you are uniquely qualified to deliver such value-added services. There will be less need for high-priced, outside consultants...no theorists from academia...no so-called experts from corporate America. The payoff for you and your customers will be the redefining of value instead of negotiating price.

PART TWO

THE TRANSITION

CHAPTER 3

THE SEVEN LAWS
OF DSR CONSULTING

LAW ONE
UNDERSTAND YOUR CUSTOMER'S CORE BUSINESS:
DEVELOP A "SUCCESS PROFILE"

The first rule in consulting is to understand your customers and their market position within a geographical area or "neighborhood." What segment are they in—theme, fine dining, casual/mid-scale, or quick-service? How does each of their particular operations work, and what are their problems, challenges, and opportunities? For example, a quick-service restaurant will have a high demand for convenience products to be prepared by entry-level, mostly unskilled, labor. A white-tablecloth restaurant, on the other hand, will have highly skilled workers in the kitchen and will be very demanding about quality. Much of this will be intuitive, based upon your existing business relationships and what you have heard on the street from other suppliers, your customers' competitors, and from the market at large.

It is important that you have a frame of reference from which to draw initial conclusions about what your best approach might be for establishing product sales activity or expanding it. From the very first moment, give your customers the impression that you have an accurate perspective on their menu and their position within the market. Customers want to feel that you have taken the time and devoted the energy to customize product solutions exclusively for them. This extra effort will immediately establish you as different from most other sales representatives who call on them. It is the first step in defining yourself as a consultant, not just another salesperson. You will place yourself on an entirely different level, characterized by a thorough knowledge of your customer's business, and a willingness to serve the needs of that business.

LAW TWO
PROVIDE PRODUCT SOURCING

As a consultant, you want to become the ultimate source for new products—a veritable "walking, talking encyclopedia." Be the person your customer turns to for every possible product, supply or service. Be the expert on existing product alternatives, as well as on the specifications and appropriate applications for virtually everything in your product line.

The strongest interest your customers will have will be new products, including items you may not carry. They want to know what's new, exciting and different. Once you have developed a profile of their concepts—price points, market positioning, food/merchandising focus, degree of sophistication, etc.—matching up new products with your customers will become the most exciting and challenging part of your consulting role. Great examples of products that DSR's introduced to me include Holsum's Breakthrough Salad Oil, Stanislaus Tomato Magic, and Nabisco's Grey Poupon Dijon Mustard as a base for a Caesar salad dressing.

Let's say a customer needs Armenian cracker bread for a smoked fish appetizer. As a product resource and a consultant, your job is to be thorough in your research of all food manufacturers, even if your company doesn't sell Armenian cracker bread. Explore transportation options, cost parameters, plate presentation options, portions, shelf life, volume discounts, pack size, minimum orders, payment terms, and so on. Sometimes, submitting a recommendation for a special serving accouterment, ramekin, plate, rarebit, or dish—one with a little style and visual punch—can provide the right "packaging" for a menu item to become a giant success.

Provide a standardized product specification sheet, including all of the above information. If you have the capabilities, you might also include a fully described recipe. This product specification sheet should have your company logo at the top of the page to continually reinforce your customers' "top-of-mind" awareness of your company as their partner for profit. As often and as regularly as possible, you should bring in new product samples for the executive chef or general manager. Encourage tastings by the staff or by selected patrons in a focus group environment. You'll find that your customers will begin to anticipate your visits, and will be more positively inclined to consider the product samples you have suggested.

You are uniquely qualified to provide trend analysis and new product introductions, and you need to be ever alert to unique food applications, innovative plate presentations, and exciting recipe concepts. As the market becomes increasingly competitive, your customers will become more insistent about exploring new ideas and experimenting with different products.

LAW THREE
DELIVER MARKET INTELLIGENCE

All of your customers, within any market segment, can develop a tendency to become "operations driven." They forget that they are in business to serve their guests, and often fail to remember that they are demand driven, not supply driven. Frequently, they become too focused on the messages they send through TV, radio and the newspaper. Instead, they should be listening to and focusing on their guests.

As an active salesperson, you travel extensively throughout your sales territory. You have become an expert on local, state and national trends. You know the competition— who is successful, who isn't, and why. You know who just opened up for business and who is on the verge of closing. This is part of the reason why you are so ideally suited for an ongoing consulting role. You know who your customers' customers are.

There is a useful rule of thumb that defines your customer's local market as being within 5 miles or a 15-minutes drive time of their facility. Your customers should be working to attract more patrons from their immediate trading area—from their own backyard. To help in this process, create a map of each customer's local market—the area within the 5-mile/15-minute guideline (Figure 9). Then, encourage them to focus on the business potential of this "neighborhood." Counsel them to concentrate on local, store-based, direct-response promotions, and discourage them from spending money on media that reaches beyond their local market, beyond the people with the highest potential to become their patrons.

FIGURE 9

YOUR CUSTOMER'S NEIGHBORHOOD

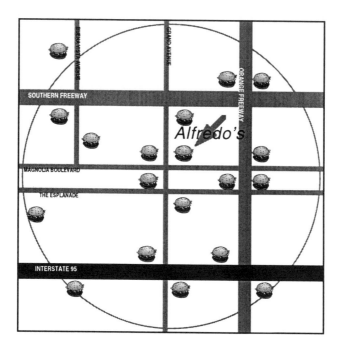

The same criteria should be applied when making decisions about supporting community activities. Help your customers understand that this support should be concentrated within their defined trading area. We generally consider our community to be larger than the five miles surrounding our home or business. Your customers, however, must be cautioned to resist this concern for the extended community, especially if such involvement exhausts precious resources of time and money. Just like charity, community involvement begins at home.

LAW FOUR
READ THE TRADE PUBLICATIONS OPERATORS READ

Most of your customers subscribe to foodservice trade publications—Restaurant Business, FoodService Director, Restaurant Hospitality, Restaurants & Institutions, Nation's Restaurant News—to name a few. But most operators don't read these valuable publications as frequently and as thoroughly as they should. The next time you're in the office of one of your customers, look for that tell-tale stack of magazines. You know what I'm talking about, you may even have a pile in your own office collecting dust. If your customers don't have the time to read the trades and benefit from the news and information they contain, then perhaps you should do it for them. It's one of the easiest ways to develop "value-added" customer service. Make operator-oriented publications a part of your regular reading.

Imagine if someone cared enough about you to read distribution and sales-oriented magazines and clip articles that could be of interest and benefit to you. How do you feel when someone takes the time out of their busy day to do something for you that is totally unexpected and beyond the call of duty?

Operator magazines can also position you as the "expert." They offer a tremendous opportunity to give your customers valuable new ideas, facts, trends, and programs. This is what consulting is all about. And, if you're ever in doubt about what topics are top of mind with your customers, trade publications can give you the information you need.

The point is, to be an effective consultant, you must clearly understand the world of your customer. This thorough knowledge imparts great credibility to your thoughts and suggestions. It helps put the "stamp of authority" on your service.

When you read this book or distribution trade

magazines, you are looking for ideas and information that will help one person—you. When you read foodservice publications for information, you are looking for 20, 30, maybe 60 different people—your customers. Every page will have something relevant for at least one of your accounts.

Clip all articles and editorials, as well as product, equipment and recipe columns. Then, when you have accumulated a thick stack of good material, go through it again and decide which articles would be most appropriate for each of your operator customers.

FIGURE 10

A NOTE FROM A DSR

Regency Distributing Company

Thought of your new menu when

I read this. Let's talk next time

I come in.   Bob

Robert Crow

(530) 345-0212 direct line

For example, an editorial on establishing a tip credit might fit the needs of an operator who is currently involved in state legislation through his restaurant association. A "how to" article on setting up delivery capability for a quick-service operation would be welcomed by one of your customers who competes with Pizza Hut and Domino's. A recipe for Pasta Primavera, made with ingredients you source in advance, might be the perfect item for a healthcare customer looking for ideas to utilize trim from raw vegetable preparation.

Send articles like these to the decision-makers at your accounts. Have 3 x 5 stationery cards printed with your company logo, your name and phone number (Figure 10). These informal cards are perfect for a quick, hand-written note and are more professional than a post-it note. If you're organized, it won't take a lot of time to jot a personal note and slip the card and article into an envelope. I guarantee, the impact will be very positive.

Take the ideas of the experts, and present them as possible solutions for your customers. Show them that you really walk the talk of "selling solutions, not just products." This is a value-added service that tells your customers you care. It also keeps you focused and up to date with the changes in the marketplace. You will gain professionally and financially. And the bonus is that you will have accomplished this by building a relationship and providing a value-added benefit for your customers.

LAW FIVE
OFFER "HANDS-ON" IMPLEMENTATION OPTIONS

It's no secret that most foodservice operators work long hours under immense pressures. The challenge of selecting a primary distributor can be a simple or complex process—depending on their priorities. For each customer, the priorities will be different: price, delivery schedules, product affiliations, brand loyalties, or personal friendships. You can give yourself a distinct advantage if you provide "turnkey" solutions to your customers, ones that take much of the work out of creating new profit centers on the menu.

Do as much work for your customers as you possibly can. Develop a clear, comprehensive format (Figure 11) in which to present your product-line options, menu-item alternatives, and marketing ideas. This format outlines the most important information associated with the introduction of a new menu item, or the reworking of an existing item. Put it all on your company's letterhead, with your business card attached to provide a reminder that this value-added service came from you.

Let's look at some of the turnkey information you can provide. A significant, untapped resource in the foodservice business is the vast amount of data, resources, ideas, and marketing collateral available from food manufacturers like Nabisco, Nestlé or Dreyer's Grand Ice Cream. Table tents, menu clip-on's, POP displays, recipe fold-outs, and other assorted promotional materials often go unused. Many operators don't know how to integrate such visual merchandising collateral into their operating configuration. They may lack the imagination and creativity necessary to develop really effective promotional displays, server selling techniques, and interior POP material.

FIGURE 11

A DSR INTRODUCES A NEW MENU ITEM

REGENCY LTD. Food Service Co.

ITEM: 6 oz. Smoked Boneless Chicken Breast

CODE: 11-9600

PACK: B 10# frozen

DESCRIPTION:

1-10oz. hardwood smoked premium quality chicken breast. Can be served cold. Ideally suited for pasta.

PREPARATION TECHNIQUE:

Sauté julienned strips with wild mushrooms and garlic. Finish with red wine and serve over angel hair pasta.

SUGGESTED CHINA: Syracuse 2011 Adobe

SUGGESTED GARNISH:

Sliced pears, lentil pine nut salad, parsley

SELLING PRICE: $ 7.95

COSTING:
Base Cost: $ 1.79
Garnish: $ 0.88
Total: $ 2.67

FOOD COST: 33.6%

GROSS PROFIT CONTRIBUTION: $ 5.28

Keep yourself current on the vast variety of merchandising material available to your customers, as well as the different types of credits they can use if they elect to experiment with suppliers' promotions. Pay special attention to garnishes, like those proposed in Figure 11, as well as suggested china, recommended preparation techniques, item names and descriptions, proposed price points, and estimated gross profits. This valuable detail will assist your customer in analyzing the profit of the new item as compared to other items on their menu. If your suggestion for a smoked chicken breast is fully costed and introduced in a "turnkey" fashion, it will have a better chance of making it onto the menu. In this new age of consultative selling, you don't just sell solutions—you provide comprehensive, completely detailed and costed profit opportunities. Don't be afraid to present a great branded product—a center-of-the-plate item—with the right visual punch to drive sales for you and your customers. It's so simple and so effective!

By using a format such as this, you have not only addressed the critical specification questions about a new menu item, but you have begun to guide your client in the right direction—toward thinking of a menu item on the basis of its value-perception pricing opportunity, and its potential for gross profit contribution. You've begun to teach your operator customer a new approach to profitability through the menu.

LAW SIX
BECOME A CUSTOMER OF YOUR CUSTOMERS

When you visit your customers' operations as a guest, you gain added credibility as a consultant. You show a vote of confidence in the menus you have helped develop, and you earn the right to offer constructive criticism or heaps of praise. You may also act as an informal "mystery shopper" who provides an outside perspective and honest input about food quality, plate presentation, flavor, portion size, service, and price points.

Leave your business card with a short handwritten greeting, and follow up later with a personal note. The personal touch is the key to this selling tip, and keeps you and your distributor company "top-of-mind." It's a very simple approach, but it always works, and it makes it easier to talk about the menu when you have a personal, as well as a professional, point of view. Have some fun with this idea, and make it a regular part of your selling program.

LAW SEVEN
PROVIDE TOOLS

A shortage of time and money is a constant worry of nearly every foodservice operator. You have a chance to promote and expand your consulting relationships by providing your customers with new and innovative time saving tips and cost-control techniques. Maintain a file of tips and techniques that you learn from observing operators, both successful and unsuccessful. Such publications as Success, Inc., and Entrepreneur are excellent sources of tools and pertinent information, packaged for easy reading and application. Implementing these concepts can make an immediate impact on your customer's bottom line.

Use these tools to address some common and costly problems faced by your customer. For example, a significant rise in food costs can occur when receiving procedures are not followed correctly. How?

- It is noon, the peak of the lunch rush. A delivery of $800 worth of meat arrives at the back door, and the manager is on the floor serving his guests. Instead of summoning the manager, or weighing the order to make sure the invoice is correct, the dishwasher just accepts the delivery and signs his name.

- A local hamburger chain prides itself on the fresh rolls it serves. The assistant unit manager, however, initials a delivery invoice for day-old bread without checking the order for freshness and correct texture.

- The purchasing agent at the local university has become friends with one of his delivery drivers. After learning his delivery schedule, he arranges to sign for all of the deliveries without noting the shortages in the beverage cases. With the kick-backs they get from selling the shorted items to someone else, they share a pair of season tickets for the local NBA team.

Each of these situations costs your customer a great deal in quality, time and money. Figure 12 shows an idea taken from a trade publication that could be the first step in eliminating this type of problem. It is a receiving procedures acknowledgment, and provides an easy-to-understand list of the rules for authorizing deliveries at the back door. It requires an employee's signature, making each one accountable for following the rules. No more excuses when the procedure isn't followed correctly.

A tool like this is only one example of how you can be of value-added assistance to your customers. There are thousands of operating tips, cost-control concepts, management systems, kitchen checklists, and foodservice-oriented ideas available. You need only edit or customize these ideas as appropriate, put them on your company's letterhead, and present them as gifts to your partners in profit. The tools and solutions you can offer will help your customers run their businesses far more efficiently, save or make money, and solve many of their operational problems. This "top-of-mind awareness" will help reposition you as a consultant and a source of solutions, not just an order taker.

These are the core concepts to build upon with your customers. Much like blocking and tackling in football, consistent execution along with professional follow-through will insure growing market share for you and your company. As you begin to adopt this type of a consulting mind-set, your

FIGURE 12

RECEIVING PROCEDURES ACKNOWLEDGMENT

REGENCY LTD. Food Service Co.

All product purchased by this restaurant will be received according to the following procedures:

√   Always check the actual items received against a copy of the purchase order or order sheet master. Check for quantity, size, brand and quality.

√   Always weigh any items that are costed by the pound.

√   Physically count any items that are costed by the piece: line items, produce, liquors, etc. EVERY TIME!

√   If items are not correct, bring it to the attention of the driver/salesperson immediately.

√   For substitutions or incorrect items, have the driver/salesperson initial the entry along with your own initials.

I understand the above receiving procedures.

_____

Employee Signature   **Date**

customers will see that you are a cut above the rest of the salespeople. Over time, these seven laws will foster credibility, solidify the personal connection, increase sales, and lower costs.

Once you establish a consulting relationship with a customer and begin the process of introducing and coordinating various aspects of menu-marketing, merchandising, and engineering, something very exciting and interesting occurs. Your customers start returning your calls. Appointments become easier to set. Meeting times become more flexible. You are treated with greater professional courtesy.

Eventually, you will become one of the "selling elite," one of the 20% that sells 80% of the products to the foodservice community. To achieve this will require discipline and consistency, but your customers will elevate you above your competitors and differentiate your products from others. Charles Revson, founder of Revlon used to say, "We don't sell cosmetics, we sell hope." Much in the same way, you don't sell products, you sell solutions!

CHAPTER 4

THE BUSINESS PROFILE

Good consultants always do their homework about their clients before formulating any opinions or recommending any changes to them. I like to develop a simple "success profile" of each client to help me develop a balanced perspective about their situation. I look for insights to help customize my selling approach to their circumstances, and at the same time assess their financial health, management sophistication, and operational readiness.

I strongly recommend taking a structured approach to each of your customer calls, whether it's for the first or the fiftieth time. Follow a mental checklist you have outlined to form a diagnosis of your customers' potential for success. As a consultant, you must understand some of the finer points of their business from an "insider's" perspective in order to build new credibility. Many of you are former operators yourselves. How often do you draw upon your prior experience when presenting your credentials to your customers? Here are some crucial pieces of information all DSR's should obtain for making a diagnosis:

1. Look at a customer's "time in grade," or his number of years in business. 75% of all restaurant failures occur in the first two years of business. Each of your prospects represents a certain amount of risk, while at

the same time offering a certain amount of potential. Be mindful of this when evaluating your approach to sales. Don't be too quick to suggest menu upgrades and other refinements until the customer's concept has begun to mature in the market.

2. What is the customer's market segment? How is the concept "positioned" relative to the market and the overall trends in the industry? For example, is the current explosion of rotisserie chicken restaurants a fad or a trend? How about '50s diners? Remember, history tends to repeat itself. Many forecasters believe that the 1990s are a rebirth of the '60s. Why else would limited-menu, drive-thru hamburger stands, such as Rally's and Checkers', be one of the hottest trends today? Or how about the return of the steakhouse?

3. What is your customer's approximate food/beverage mix? This is very significant in understanding the basic focus of a particular foodservice business. For example, in a conventional fine-dining, white-tablecloth restaurant, a 75–25 food to beverage mix is typical. However, if the alcoholic beverage component rises above 30% of total sales, it is widely held that you are now dealing with a bar/lounge or entertainment facility that serves food, as opposed to a restaurant that serves beverages. There is a marked difference in management style, marketing approach, and in the financial expectations of the owners. These operators are also perceived differently by customers, and the motivations and orientation of employees may be very different as well.

4. What is your customer's average check? By definition, the average check is: total revenues (excluding sales taxes and tips) divided by total covers served. Often, operators do not know how to calculate their average check. Here is a good opportunity to provide some basic consulting support.

    Generally speaking, operations with an average check above $15 are considered fine dining, from $7 to $15 is considered casual/family dining, and checks below $7 are considered quick service. You should know where each of your customers falls within this range. With a higher average check, there is a greater emphasis placed on service, and a more complicated preparation and delivery of menu items. There is also a greater danger of failing to meet guest expectations about food quality and value.

5. Be familiar with the local target market of each of your customers. The local market is considered to be within a 5-mile radius, or a 15-minute drive time. What are the basic demographic and psychographic factors of the local population, including average household income, most popular radio stations, types of cars driven, average expenditures for dining out, and so forth? Customer spending patterns and lifestyle characteristics are major market factors your customers should understand, and so should you.

6. Knowing whether the facility is owned or leased can give you valuable insight into the short- and long-term objectives of your customers. Operators who own their real estate tend to have a longer view of the restaurant's potential, and are more likely to

experiment with menu and marketing strategies that will solidify the restaurant's market position. Operators who lease, on the other hand, are more interested in short-term returns on investment than on devoting energy to the facility, since they will not share in the equity buildup on the real estate.

7.   What are the occupancy costs incurred by your customers? Rent/lease costs, personal and real estate property taxes, and associated insurance costs should not exceed 10% of revenues, if things are going well. As the density of the retail environment/market increases, rents go up proportionately. Shopping malls have high rents because restaurants located there have a guaranteed stream of customers. Prime free-standing or in-line locations use daily car counts as one key indicator to justify higher rents. Knowing the approximate occupancy costs provides you with an added dimension of insight into your customer's potential for success.

8.   Are your customers involved in their community? Do they operate as the "mayor of the village," working to influence local business conditions? Are they members of their state or local restaurant association, chamber of commerce, or visitors and convention bureaus? Do they sponsor youth activities or senior citizen clubs? In every neighborhood market, a grass-roots commitment to community service and involvement is a key building block for the success of any business.

9.   What is your customers' financial commitment to effective marketing activities? How much are they willing to spend on marketing, as a percentage of total

sales? The most successful restaurant concepts— whether commercial or non-commercial—are market- driven. Three percent of total sales should be the absolute minimum budgeted for marketing, and five percent is ideal.

In addition to the amount spent on marketing, what type of marketing is being done? Do your customers engage in newspaper advertising? Historically, this is the worst form of foodservice advertising. It calls for high preparation and distribution costs, and targets a large segment of the population that generally falls outside the establishment's magic 5-mile radius or 15- minute drive time. The most effective forms of marketing available to your customers are store promotions and direct-mail announcements targeted within a very local trading area or neighborhood.

Learning to develop a success profile on a new or existing customer is the first step in the transition from run-of- the-mill salesperson to consultant. Your customers will come to rely on you for a localized market perspective and an experienced, sensible approach to help them manage their businesses more successfully. This needs-assessment checklist will give you a competitive edge in understanding your customers, defining their goals and objectives, and most importantly, helping them achieve their goals.

CHAPTER 5

THE "ACID TEST"

The acid test is a surprisingly accurate method to ascertain the profit potential in a foodservice operation. To administer the acid test, take the annual sales of the foodservice operation and divide this figure by the square footage. This will give you annual sales per square foot.

For example: a foodservice facility with $1,000,000 in annual sales and a total of 2,500 square feet has annual sales of $400 per square foot ($1,000,000 \div 2,500 = 400$).

In the commercial segment, restaurants need sales of at least $300 per square foot to achieve their full profit potential. If an operation is generating less than $300/sq. ft., chances are the operation doesn't have sufficient gross sales to support its concept. In cases like this, your consulting focus should be on the top line: sales-building. This would include marketing activities, menu engineering and menu merchandising.

If the foodservice facility is currently producing more than $300/sq. ft., it probably has sufficient gross sales to support the concept. The best way to help this customer is to focus on the bottom line. You can do this by helping with improvements to operating systems, and on better cost-control techniques.

PART THREE

PRIME COST
CONTROLS

CHAPTER 6

LOWERING
DIRECT LABOR COST

Once you have conducted the "acid test" for each of your customers, compare their operation to the $300 benchmark. If revenues are over $300 per square foot, you know that their sales velocity is adequate to meet basic overhead and core costs for the restaurant or foodservice facility. Therefore, your primary focus should be on lowering your customer's prime costs. "Prime costs," located below "revenues" on the income statement (Chapter 1, Figure 4), represent roughly 63¢ spent out of each foodservice dollar in the typical restaurant operation. They are defined as food and beverage costs (expressed as "Cost Of Sales") plus direct labor cost, not including benefits.

Your customers want instant gratification—and you can provide it. First, you need to determine what your customers' problems are—what's causing them grief or losing them money. The old adage, pioneered by business guru Tom Winninger, "best customer, highest pain" is, without a doubt, a powerful philosophical principle in consultative selling.

As a consultant, you can help reduce your customer's biggest source of pain—prime costs—within a matter of weeks through the introduction of innovative, imaginative "trade secrets." These trade secrets are cost control techniques, operating systems, and management concepts that can be applied to solve problems and immediately increase profits.

Let's first look at how to address direct labor costs. Labor cost, or payroll, is the largest stand-alone, controllable expense that an operator has to cover. In addition, payroll taxes, benefits, and workers' compensation add an average of 20% to every payroll dollar, so that a $5 per hour wage becomes $6 per hour. These are hidden costs that can sting an operator. Remember the "magic nickel"? It only takes a slight miscalculation in labor scheduling to wipe out that nickel. Effectively managing labor, on the other hand, can yield two nickels. As a consultant, you can present new cost-saving ideas to your customers. The following scenario illustrates a way labor cost controls can be directly and successfully addressed.

CONTROLLING EMPLOYEE TURNOVER IS THE KEY

Samantha "Sam" Marston had finally done it. After 12 years of working through the ranks of the Red Rock family restaurant chain, she is a general manager with her own store in Tucson, Arizona. Red Rock is always very concerned about profit and loss accountability. They give their unit managers tremendous autonomy and latitude in managing their $1 million-a-year restaurants. Unfortunately for Sam, after only eight months in her new job as manager, she had a serious labor problem. Sam's competition was stealing away her best employees. In some cases the competition was offering a dollar-an-hour more for the same job. Sam is at her wit's end covering shifts, working 80 hours a week, and searching desperately for some fresh ideas to keep her remaining loyal and capable employees from being lured away by her competitors.

What time-tested "trade secret" could Sam's DSR use to help solve her problem? A start would be to have Sam calculate her Employee Turnover Ratio (ETR). The ETR simply measures the percentage of the labor force that changed, or "turned over," during a year. As the labor crisis worsens, the ETR will become the ultimate report card for management effectiveness.

Here's how it works:

The Employee Turnover Ratio (ETR) is:

W-2's Issued minus Number of Employees Working at Year End
[divided by] Number of Employees Working at Year End

Example

140 W-2's issued with 80 Employees Working at Year End =

$$\frac{140 - 80}{80}$$

ETR = 0.75 or 75%

In this example, the Red Rock issued 140 W-2's and had 80 employees at the end of the year—an Employee Turnover Ratio (ETR) of 0.75 or 75%. This means that three-fourths of the labor force changed during one year. This may seem high, but actually, it's a relatively low ETR. In the hospitality and foodservice industry, the annual average is consistently over 100%.

And turnover is expensive! Direct costs of employee turnover include: lower productivity, recruiting costs, training (costs and time), theft, and administrative and payroll processing. The average cost to turn over an employee in a mid-scale operation is over $500. Indirect costs of employee turnover include: lower customer satisfaction, lack of consistency in service and product, low employee morale, scheduling headaches and last minute personnel substitutions.

We haven't even considered what the manager's time is worth. Most owners and managers will tell you that the 80/20 law applies to managing—they spend 80% of their time managing 20% of their employees. The same 20% that is constantly turning over. What kind of time allocation does this leave for good employees? Frequently good employees are neglected, and the cycle begins. A potential "superstar" becomes a dissatisfied employee, and then a former employee.

What does this mean to your customer? Employee turnover causes havoc with operations. Service, quality, portion control, plate presentation, and guest satisfaction are just of few of the casualties. Too many new employees means inconsistent execution. It signals instability at a time when today's fickle customer has too many choices. Think about this fact: 70% of those individuals surveyed who said they would not return to a restaurant cited a bad interaction with an employee as the reason.

To avoid becoming one of the statistics, operators will have to recruit, train, and motivate higher quality employees. And that will cost money. Your customers will tell you they can't afford to pay higher wages, much less offer the benefits that the health care industry and retail segment are using to lure foodservice employees away. But they are spending the money already.

Remember the $500 it costs to turn over each employee? If your customer turns over 50 employees in a year, it is costing them $25,000. That's $25,000 that could be invested in existing employees. It's no wonder they move on to other jobs or industries where they can receive good wages, benefits, and ongoing training. It's no wonder that operators are having such a difficult time recruiting quality employees. Yet, as obvious as this seems, operators are not accustomed to thinking this way, and they lose good employees.

There's only one way to recruit and keep the superstars: Training. The time spent training 60 new employees could be better spent teaching advanced skills, techniques, and management practices to existing employees. Why spend training time and money repeating the "Introductory Course"? If employees don't continue developing skills that can lead to greater productivity and higher wages, operators will simply be training employees for their competition.

You can offer tips on how to formalize training programs. It's easy to get information from your state restaurant association, or the Education Foundation of the National Restaurant Association. Many of your own companies have spent thousands of dollars on "partnering" programs to deal with these fundamental business issues. Maybe you just haven't figured out a way to make the connection to your customer's operation. Teaching your customer to use the Employee Turnover Ratio could be that simple connection—a way to open the door to consultative selling.

CHAPTER 7

LOWERING COST OF SALES

In addition to labor costs, attention should be directed toward to your customers' cost of sales, or food and beverage costs. The following are two examples of operators with a specific cost of sales problem. In each case, the DSR viewed the problem as an opportunity, and was able to provide a trade secret that was on target.

CONTROLLING FOOD COSTS –
A BLINDING FLASH OF THE "OBVIOUS"

Randell's Seafood Restaurant is located in Ocean City, Maryland. It is a large, brand new operation, open for one year, and highly successful. Food cost fluctuations are a constant problem for Jerry Cox, the kitchen manager. He suspects all the normal causes—theft, waste, poor recipe adherence, inexact portioning, and improper preparation techniques. Jerry is frustrated because one week the food cost is 34%, and the next it's 41% or 26%. There's no consistency or stability. What can his DSR recommend that might be of help?

In consulting—or operational problem-solving—the key is to look for the simplest and easiest-to-implement solution. There are many reasons for this:

- Time is your most precious resource, so look for "quick fixes" first.

- You will be providing motivation by taking all the obstacles out of their way.

- You should focus on steps that are consistent with existing work patterns. "Ride the horse in the direction it's already going."

- Simple lessons are most easily remembered and retained. Crawl before you walk.

A baseline needs to be established to judge food cost fluctuations. The first step would be to determine what Jerry's food cost should be. This is called a theoretical food cost. It is based on three factors: correct and accurate recipe costing, adherence to proper portioning, and consistent price points. A theoretical food cost is calculated by multiplying the cost of each recipe by the number sold. This is calculated over a specified period of time, usually one week. A detailed discussion on recipe costing can be found in Chapter Nine.

Once the food cost baseline has been established, it's time to give Jerry an idea he can implement easily, one which will cause an immediate change in both his food cost and in the thinking of his staff. Tell Jerry to remove all of the garbage cans from the production area. Eliminate those 50-gallon monstrosities-on-wheels. In their place, substitute a number of clear Lexan food boxes with full-sized, six-inch deep pans. These tubs can be "racked" on a baker's cart (Figure 13).

Food waste, such as trim from the fruit and vegetables, meat cutting, and fish filleting, is now accumulated and stored in the food boxes. Each production and preparation worker should have his or her own tub for their trim. When a tub is filled, a plastic lid is placed on top, along with the prep worker's name. Then the full box is then placed on the baker's cart, and the worker takes another empty box.

FIGURE 13

A TOOL FOR COST CONTROL

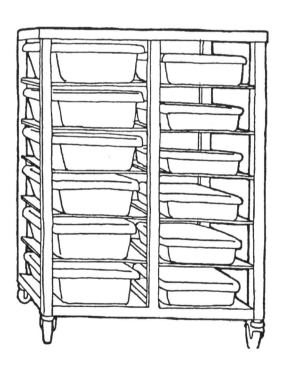

At the end of the shift, before the prep workers leave, Jerry or his assistant kitchen manager should take five minutes to quickly examine the contents of each full food box. A quick inspection will tell whether preparation techniques and knife skills are being followed, and if established yields are being met. Jerry will have the complete attention of the kitchen staff as he begins to rummage through each worker's production trim, asking questions such as...

- Are the carrots being trimmed at the end or one inch from the end?

- Is the pineapple being "skinned" with the proper knife, one-quarter inch below the skin, as the preparation specifications state?

- Is there excess trim from the meat cutting or fish filleting?

- Are yield sheets being filled out properly and submitted for review?

The answers to these questions depend on what I call the "end-product" perspective. That is, can you measure what you manage? Can Jerry or his fellow kitchen supervisors quickly and efficiently observe whether proper knife skills and techniques are being applied to the breakdown, slicing and dicing of raw food products? Once the visual inspection is completed, the production waste is transferred to trash bags and deposited in the dumpster.

During this process, a prep worker undergoes a bit of "behavioral modification." They simply cannot hide from the results of their work. It's on display for everyone to see and to grade. This "garbage-can theory" precipitates significant changes in the efficiency of a kitchen operation. Simply being aware of the waste produced in the kitchen caused the staff to become cost conscious. As a result food costs will start to decline.

Proper techniques will be employed when the managers are directly observing the preparation process. But most kitchens are so busy that direct supervision of all production or cooking activities is virtually impossible. The elimination of the garbage cans in the production area forces the production staff to be directly responsible for yields and proper preparation techniques.

A suggestion like this, offered to a frustrated kitchen manager such as Jerry, will earn immediate praise, and will create a new sense of appreciation for the DSR's insight and wisdom. The "garbage-can theory," and other ideas like it, are dramatic ways to introduce your consultative skills and reinforce your commitment to helping your customers improve their profitability. The idea truly is a blinding flash of the obvious.

CONTROLLING BEVERAGE COSTS – THE BIN CARD

Boston's famous No-Name bar is located in an historic alley just off the Common. The No-Name is a Boston landmark, serving generous cocktails and a choice of three lunch or dinner entrées. The No-Name generates annual revenues of $2.5 million, based upon sales of $50,000/week. Bar sales account for 40% of all revenues. This has helped to insure profitability for the restaurant's new owner, Terry Mahony. When the family-owned No-Name was sold to Terry, he had never before been in the bar and restaurant business. Before Terry assumed ownership, the restaurant had a high food cost—over 50%. Its beverage costs, however, had traditionally remained a low 25%. During the first six months of his ownership, his beverage cost began to gradually inch upward. When this cost finally hit 30%, Terry became seriously concerned.

What "trade secret" could Terry employ as a solution to this problem? The answer was relatively simple. Terry's DSR simply asked if the No-Name had a control system to manage the beverage inventory. The inevitable answer was "no." His DSR suggested implementing a perpetual inventory system.

FIGURE 14

THE BEVERAGE INVENTORY NOTATION (BIN) CARD

Jack Daniels Black Label, 750 ml			
Date	Received	Issued To Bar	Balance On-Hand
Monday 1/22			= 6
Monday 1/29	+12	– 1	= 17
Wednesday 2/11		– 1	= 16
Friday 2/20		– 4	= 12

With this system, ongoing records for each beverage are kept on Beverage Inventory Notation (BIN) cards (Figure 14), which describe the brand and bottle size of each item. As new stock is received or bottles are issued to the bar, the information is logged on the BIN card, along with the date of each transaction. This simple, manual approach allows managers to "spot check" the storeroom inventory on a daily basis, and review working inventories with bartenders. Empty or broken bottles should be disposed of after the manager has made sure the inventory is accurate. Just by implementing the control system, your customer will see improvement.

Again, providing a solution is often no more than identifying a possible direction for cost controls, or stimulating the owner to act when the cost percentage becomes excessive. Remember, keep your eyes open and ask questions. That's often all it takes to get you started.

Bartenders can accumulate, over the course of a shift, a significant amount of cash from payments not "rung up." For example, in an average bar or cocktail lounge operation, by the end of the shift this excess cash could be $50 or more. The problem for the thieving bartender is that he has to somehow keep track in his head of the total amount of cash skimmed. For example, if a bartender accumulates $40 in cash that has not been rung up, the typical behavior is to only take $30—to psychologically "cover your tracks" by taking less than you have actually skimmed. But keeping an accurate account of what has been skimmed is difficult to do. A bartender who is stealing can usually be identified by monitoring a pattern of overages, as shown in Figure 14.

PART FOUR

SALES BUILDING

CHAPTER 8

THE MENU

THE PUREST FORM OF THE MARKETING PLAN

Now to the other side of the acid test. We have examined ways that you can help customers with revenues exceeding $300 per square foot. By implementing operating systems and cost-control techniques, they can get relief from the pressure of ever-tightening margins. But what about your customers with annual sales of less than $300/sq. ft.? These customers need sales building techniques, and here is your greatest opportunity as a DSR and a consultative seller. The easiest and fastest way to build revenues to the $300/sq. ft. mark is through the menu. Your ability to analyze your customer's menu will build your credibility, and differentiate you from the conventional order takers.

Whether your customer is an independent or a chain, a high-volume dinner house, fast-food chili shop, hot-doggery, or corporate cafeteria, your most powerful connection with your customer is the menu. Historically underestimated by DSR's and misunderstood by restaurateurs, the menu is the cornerstone of all foodservice or hospitality activities. It is the purest form of the marketing plan, linked as much to marketing as to operations. Actually, I see the menu as the bridge between marketing and operations. It is a concrete symbol of the foodservice and hospitality business. We are all familiar with the menu as an integral part of the dining experience.

The menu sets the tone for every operation, whether quick-service, mid-range/casual, or fine-dining. It defines the degree of management effort, labor intensity, and technological complexity associated with the delivery of food to the customer. For non-commercial operators, the menu allows a better use of budget dollars, improves available capital, and lowers the reliance on outside subsidy. In the non-commercial marketplace, a $90-billion business, food cost is always a major point of concern and contention.

All of this affects the profit potential in a multitude of ways—from energy cost to china breakage, from training protocols to guest comment cards, from number of table turns to uniform expense. The menu is the connective tissue that holds the entire restaurant together. Nothing happens that in some way is not directly or indirectly affected by the menu.

The menu is the ultimate foundation of a successful restaurant. The menu is a visual translation of the food being offered. In a way, it is a product brochure. The menu is the centerpiece of the guest dining experience. It establishes expectations the food will ultimately have to fulfill in order to satisfy customers and build repeat business. It creates the spark that sets word-of-mouth advertising glowing for the establishment. Remember, a happy customer tells at least three people about his or her wonderful dining experience. An unhappy customer, however, will tell twelve. We have to accept the fact that restaurant bashing is one of America's favorite pastimes.

To fully appreciate the critical role the menu plays in the success of your customer's operation, you must consider the economic climate. Since the mid-to-late-'80s, inflation has been relatively mild. Nonetheless, all operators today, whether commercial or non-commercial, are affected by the lackluster economy and the proliferation of new competition. These marketing realities have kept menu prices down. At the same time, however, costs continue to increase, resulting in a painful price squeeze and a slow, agonizing downward slide of profits.

So, where do these operators turn for help to escape the mounting cost-price spiral that they find themselves in? They to turn to you, the DSR, and to your company. You're expected to sharpen your pencil and slice off a few extra points to help your customers survive. You don't have any more price reductions to give, so your company turns to the manufacturer. And on and on it goes, round and round, the vicious cycle of selling on price, rather than value. As a consultant, however, you have positioned yourself to sell value—to move away from price by concentrating your energies on product solutions and operational answers to your customer's problems.

The menu, of course, is a means to this end. Every operator's objective is to achieve higher sales, using the menu in one of four ways:

1.   Raise the average check. Create a broader selection.

2.   Increase the frequency of visits. Increased diversity attracts customers back more frequently, driving sales upward.

3.   Increase the party size. A great menu stimulates guests to bring friends and larger parties to share in the wonderful dining experience.

4. Attract new customers. The menu is a powerful selling tool when properly merchandised and strategically distributed through appropriate channels.

What are the important technical ideas, design concepts, and profit principles associated with the menu? First, it's important to know that people don't read menus—they scan them. The average guest spends less than three minutes reading a menu and studying the choices. It makes you wonder about the effectiveness of the five-to-ten page menus designed to showcase the talent of the chef. Eating out is a social activity, as well as a need to put gas in the tank. Most customers are either caught up in conversation within a group, or they're anxious to dig into the food. Today's guests have become accustomed to television, music videos, and motion pictures that feature quick, colorful and stimulating images. They don't have time to read.

Time has become the currency of the '90s. Two-job families, latch-key kids, and the proliferation of convenience foods from frozen pizza to pre-cooked turkey dinners have seriously influenced eating patterns. The consumer is overwhelmed by the multitude of images and messages received every day, and the choices these produce.

As a result, the menu has become a hybrid between a 30-second television commercial and print advertisement from People Magazine. Publications like this are rich in visual images, color photographs, short articles, clipped headlines, and interesting call-out boxes. The menu has taken on the same form and function. The visual package is perfect for today's busy consumer with a shortage of time. It's designed to catch the eye, project an image to the subconscious, and then cause the diner to make a quick, subliminal decision about what to order.

Have you heard of the subliminal imaging that was done in movie theaters in the 1950s? A frame or two of hot buttered popcorn was spliced into the film, not visible long enough to be noticed by the conscious mind. The result? A giant rush to the snack counter to buy popcorn. The manipulation of images influences the behavior of the customer. Menu design offers a similar, yet ethical opportunity to influence the purchasing decisions of the guest.

When guests look at the menu, their vision follows a predictable path, searching for a point of visual interest, a splash of color, a different shape or image, pattern or texture. Polished, well-designed print merchandising techniques can lead them to select certain items—hopefully ones that offer a more favorable profit margin than others. The objective is to entice and seduce the customer, through creative menu development, to buy what your customer wants to sell.

Retailers have known and understood this principle for years. Department stores place cosmetic counters near the main entrance because cosmetics are impulse purchases, they attract shoppers, and they are high-profit items. Grocery stores use advanced psychology and hard data when slotting products and assigning shelf space.

So, why should selling items on a menu be any different? It's time to throw out the conventional wisdom surrounding menu design and development, and substitute a new, outside-of-the-box kind of thinking to take us profitably into the 21st century. For DSR's, this means rethinking the way center-of-the-plate items are sold. You're not just selling a food item anymore. You're selling menu design, style, and format. It will impact the number of these center-of-the-plate items ordered. The end goal is to gain a more favorable profit margin.

Consider that the average casual or full- service restaurant will serve 150,000 customers per year with an average check of $8 per person. This produces annual sales of $1,200,000. For each of the 150,000 times that a restaurant patron opens the menu during a given year, 150,000 marketing opportunities occur. 150,000 dining experiences can potentially be influenced by design and merchandising features, such as color, pattern, typeface and size, layout, and choice of words or themes. Through creative and innovative menu design, you and your customer can affect one-third of the dining choices made by diners. And, if each of those 50,000 choices results in 10¢ additional profit, you will have contributed a significant amount of extra profit to the establishment—$5,000 to be exact. You will have handed your operator customer a gift of $5,000, which should put you head and shoulders above your competitors.

Your credibility will be instantaneous. Once you understand how easy it is to use the menu as a strategic tool to increase your customers' sales and profits, selling will become secondary and consulting will become your primary focus.

Now, let's go find those 50,000 dimes.

CHAPTER 9

FUNDAMENTAL
RECIPE COSTING

You can create a gift of knowledge that will result in a $5,000 profit for your customer. But such a positive result comes only when your customers understand the inherent profit potential within their menus. The first step toward this understanding is knowing the cost of each menu item. Your customer must be able to perform basic recipe costing. As a consultant, you can offer your expertise to help develop a useful working model.

Recipe costing is typically done using a simple "recipe explosion" format. This can be done manually, but there are many software applications that can be used, as well. Good foodservice practices dictate that a kitchen manager or chef should be able to pinpoint costs through a recipe and raw ingredients breakdown. This takes time, and it's hard work, and it is necessary. A restaurant is a manufacturing facility. The major difference from conventional manufacturing is that, in a restaurant, the product is perishable and the selling is done on premises.

You and your customer should be able to take any menu item and determine the raw cost. This is done by breaking the recipe down into its component parts—

ingredients, specifications and measurements—on a Menu Item Costing Worksheet (Figure 15). This is a tool that you can easily provide for your customers.

The menu item description and cooking procedure should be included on the worksheet (Figure 16). In addition, plating and presentation techniques (center-of-plate, starch, vegetable, garnish, etc.) should be shown on a colored sketch or photograph. Why? Because line cooks are notorious for preparing items just a little bit differently. They think of it as developing their own individual "signature." But this inconsistency can destroy a restaurant's credibility. Today's discriminating patron demands consistency, whether it's a Whopper, Cheese Burrito, or Roasted Halibut with Mango Chutney.

Once your customers learn the proper technique for recipe costing, they can develop a comprehensive recipe book, complete with food costs for each of their menu items. This is the basis for the theoretical food cost that we discussed in Chapter 7.

Accurate recipe costing is the foundation for the exciting, and profitable work we will learn about in the following chapters on pricing philosophies, menu engineering and merchandising.

FIGURE 15

MENU ITEM COSTING WORKSHEET

| Menu: | | Date: | |
| Item: | | By: | |

Description:

Item ID	Qty.	Unit	Ingredient	Unit Price	Cost
					'

			Total Cost	
			Menu Price	
			Gross Profit	
			Food Cost %	

Cooking Procedure:

FIGURE 16

COMPLETED MENU ITEM COSTING WORKSHEET

Menu:	DINNER	Date:	5/2/91

Item:	SCALLOPS SAUSALITO	By:	T. BRUCE

Description:

Tender scallops poached in white wine with butter, garlic, shallots, mushrooms and green onions. Simmered in a rich béchamel sauce and served on a bed of rice and fresh vegetables.

Item ID	Qty.	Unit	Ingredient	Unit Price	Cost
SHE514	1.0	each	Scallop Portion-7oz.	2.60	2.60
SSI133	4.0	ounce	Béchamel Sauce	0.08	0.32
DAI115	1.0	ounce	Butter Solids-unsalted	0.07	0.07
PRO102	2.0	ounce	Mushrooms-medium	0.15	0.30
PRO113	0.1	bunch	Onions-green	0.03	0.00
PRO137	0.2	ounce	Garlic-fresh	0.03	0.01
PRO154	0.6	ounce	Shallots-fresh	0.03	0.02
WIN100	2.0	ounce	Wine-house white	0.05	0.10
SSI121	4.0	ounce	Rice-cooked	0.12	0.48
GRO428	0.1	ounce	Pepper, white ground	0.39	0.04
SSI502	1.0	each	Dinner Package	1.50	1.50

	Total Cost	5.44
	Menu Price	15.95
	Gross Profit	10.51
	Food Cost %	34.1%

Cooking Procedure:

In saucepan over medium heat, mix white wine, scallops, shallots, garlic, mushrooms, and salt & pepper to taste. Simmer until scallops appear white in color, leaving 1 ounce of liquid in the pan. Add béchamel, green onion and butter; simmer for 2 minutes more until a medium consistency is reached. Serve in a large ceramic casserole dish on a bed of rice, piling scallop mixture in the middle; pour remaining sauce in pan over the top. Sprinkle lightly with paprika (for color). Serve with fresh vegetables on a large oval platter. Garnish with orange wheel and sprig of fresh parsley.

CHAPTER 10

PERCENTAGE TARGET MYOPIA

A.K.A. "FORMULA PRICING"

Once the raw cost of each menu item has been defined, the next decision the operator faces is deciding on price points. Many operators price their menu items using a standard multiplier, or a formula "mark up" on cost. This method is called formula pricing. Assume your customer has a food-cost target of 33%. The formula pricing method would set the price as follows:

$2.25 (raw cost) X 3 = $6.75 menu price

Nothing could be simpler, but the problem is that it's wrong, dead wrong. This antiquated approach is an example of percentage target myopia (PTM), or pricing nearsightedness. PTM is a reliance on food-cost percentages as the key indicator of profit performance. It impacts the thinking of almost every operator at some time during the pricing process.

Look at the example in Figure 17. The tuna sandwich has a food cost percentage of 24%. The turkey club sandwich has a food cost of 39%. Most operators would think that the tuna sandwich would be a more favorable sell, because of its lower food cost percentage. The more relevant factor, however, is an item's gross profit contribution. Even though it has a higher food cost percentage, the turkey club offers a gross profit contribution of $2.90, compared to $1.90 for the tuna sandwich. Most operators would rather have $2.90 in their pocket than $1.90.

Although the retail price for the turkey club is higher than the tuna, we will assume for comparison purposes that each sandwich is priced fairly when considering its relative value. The point here is to avoid making decisions based on food cost percentage. The important factor is the gross profit contribution. Remember, we take dollars to the bank, not percentages!

FIGURE 17

PERCENTAGE TARGET MYOPIA vs. "THE QUANTITATIVE APPROACH"				
Menu Item	Menu Price	Item Cost	Gross Profit	Cost of Sales
Reuben	$4.50	$1.45	$3.05	32%
Cheeseburger	4.50	1.56	2.94	35%
Turkey Club	4.75	1.85	2.90	39%
Danish Roll	3.50	1.14	2.36	33%
Vegetarian Pita	3.25	0.95	2.30	29%
Tuna Sandwich	2.50	0.60	1.90	24%

It must become your mission to educate your customers on the importance of gross profit contribution. Help them avoid PTM and eliminate "mark-up on cost" thinking. Reinforce your importance as a consultant, rather than a routine salesperson.

CHAPTER 11

VALUE-PERCEPTION PRICING

The pressures on food manufacturers, distributors, and operators are enormous. Operators are trying to maintain or improve their economic turf by downsizing, streamlining, and reengineering. The problem isn't new. It comes from the ever-increasing need to expand sales and profits to satisfy investors, owners and stockholders.

Manufacturers, distributors and operators are fighting over a market "pie" that enjoys a modest 2-4% profit, while the rest of the retail world enjoys 6-8%. This conflict and competition manifests itself in the form of price resistance.

What can you do to calm the waters? The answer is simple...enlarge the pie!

The goal is to create a buying environment for the restaurant guest and in the process, squeeze out a bit more profit for the operator and your company. This can be accomplished by adopting a state-of-the-art menu pricing strategy. You are uniquely qualified to teach and coach your customers through the re-pricing process.

There are five key elements to price/value response to a typical menu. By mastering a combination of these elements, you can encourage the selection of menu items that drive up the average check. These elements are:

PRODUCT KNOWLEDGE

Developing a unique selling proposition (USP) that can support a higher price point depends to some degree on the product itself. How and where a raw product is grown, processed, and positioned from a quality perspective are influencing factors, as are how the product is produced and packaged.

MERCHANDISING

Menu items should be attractively merchandised using tabletop materials, server selling, and menu inserts. A bottle of Italian Chianti with the wicker basket sleeve placed on each table, for example, will stimulate sales of wine, as well as appetizers properly "paired" with the wine.

PLATE PRESENTATION

People "eat with their eyes." Suggest specialty garnishes and accouterments that can add value. Baby potatoes, a ramekin of marinated salad, or a slice of garlic bread placed directly on top of the plate for maximum visual impact all generate the "wow" factor when the meal is placed in front of the guest.

HOT FOOD HOT AND COLD FOOD COLD

If a guest perceives quality, he is predisposed to appreciate the taste sensation that follows. If it looks good, it must be good. This is maximized by serving hot food HOT—

and I mean HOT—and cold food COLD. A server can reinforce this by warning the guest that a sizzling platter is hot, using a glove or pot holder. It's not difficult to serve a crisp salad on a chilled plate accompanied by a chilled fork, and the impact is very positive.

CHINA/SERVICE WARE, SILVERWARE, AND GLASSWARE

Subconsciously, a restaurant patron makes value-based decisions that are influenced by the serviceware, utensils, and glassware. Larger, heavier versions, which are substantial feeling and comfortable to the touch, reinforce higher price points.

Now that you understand some of the elements that mean value to the customer, what is the correct pricing discipline to adopt? How do we set prices at an incrementally higher level while delivering identical value?

Pricing should be based to some degree on the value perception of the customer. This is an intangible, often abstract combination of public perception and belief, shaped by the print, audio, and film media. This perception is often focused on branded images such as Idaho Potatoes versus a generic brand, Grey Poupon Dijon Mustard versus a no-name brand, or Montfort's Chef's Exclusive versus a standard generic brand.

Setting price points, then, must be based on value perception, and not on a formula or derivative of raw cost. Restaurant patrons rarely consider the raw cost of an item.

A few years ago I made a presentation to a large group of chefs. After concluding my remarks about the sin of formula pricing, one of the chefs raised his hand, to ask a question or offer a comment. I braced myself for the worst. This wasn't a hostile crowd, but I was in chef's territory. The gentleman grudgingly admitted that my theory was nice and made some sense, but it was totally contrary to what most chefs had been taught during their formative years.

I asked this chef what his targeted food cost was and whether he ever priced his menu items on the basis of value perception as opposed to formula-driven pricing. He responded that his target was 33% and that he did not price according to value perception.

I then asked the group to participate in a simple exercise to illustrate the concept of value-perception pricing. I asked the group to determine the cost for a cup of coffee. They decided on seven cents, plus six cents more for cream and sugar, for a total cost of 13¢.

I turned back to the chef who told me he didn't use value perception to price his menu. I said I was anxious to visit his restaurant. His must have the only white-tablecloth, fine-dining establishment in the city to sell a cup of coffee for 39¢.

After a few moment of silence, the chef responded. "No," he said slowly and deliberately. "We charge $1.25 for a cup of coffee." When I asked why, he replied, "Because we can get it. That's market price. It's what customers expect to pay."

Precisely—$1.25 is the value-perceived price for a cup of coffee. Many chefs, kitchen managers, and restaurant owners employ value-perception pricing when it's obvious, and then revert back to formula pricing when it isn't quite as clear. They are losing thousands of profit dollars as a result. This is a fabulous window of opportunity for DSR's if they can use this knowledge to challenge the typical operational mentality surrounding formula pricing.

There are three fundamental rules associated with value-perception pricing:

1. Don't make pricing decisions in a vacuum

   Pay attention to the competition within a 5-mile radius and/or 15-minute drive time of your customers' restaurants. This information will help you learn competitors' portion sizes, quality levels, cooking styles, plate presentation techniques, and price points. Use this data to show how the restaurant guest perceives value.

2. Don't allow chefs or kitchen managers to price a menu alone

   They are the people furthest from the guest. They are not as sensitive to market conditions relative to value perception. By nature, they are supply-driven since they are responsible for creating, producing and delivering the product. They're more focused on problem-solving production issues than on front-of-the-house customer challenges.

3. Utilize waiter and waitress input

   In contrast to the chef and kitchen manager, the servers are on the front line. They're closest to the guest. They know more about value-perception pricing than the results of a thousand surveys. Unlike their kitchen counterparts, servers are demand-driven because their job is to sell the product.

Here is a chance for a DSR to become a hero. Introduce your customers to the idea that their waitstaff is the most underutilized asset they have. Urge them to tap the front-line experiences of these salespeople to help determine price points that maximize gross profit contributions. Suggest that your customers systematize the gathering of opinions from waiters and waitresses. An effective way to do this is through the server focus group.

Help your customers organize a server focus group, and develop a form (Figure 18). Print a generic version on your company letterhead. It will be a reminder of your value as a consultative seller. I recommend that a focus group be held each quarter. Ask servers to describe the guests' response to selected menu items and to rate each item on a one-to-five scale, indicating whether they sense any price resistance.

If operators don't solicit the opinions of their waitstaff, they're losing a tremendous opportunity to gain meaningful, first-hand information about the selection tendencies of guests. Servers earn their livelihood "reading" guest satisfaction to maximize tip income.

There's an added bonus for allowing servers to offer their insights during a server focus group—a higher level of self-esteem and professionalism. Everyone loves to offer an opinion, and waiters and waitresses are no exception.

The information learned during a server focus group can help your customer establish price points which maximize gross profit contributions and ultimate profits. These are prices that reflect the best "value perception." The correct way to set price points using value-perception pricing is through a collaboration between the chef or kitchen manager, the front-of-the-house managers, and the waiters and waitresses. Menu-analysis meetings are effective team-building activities as well.

FIGURE 18

LUNCH MENU
SERVER FOCUS GROUP SURVEY

GUEST SATISFACTION Low High					ITEM	PRICE	RESISTANCE?	
1	2	3	4	5	Alfredo	$ 5.95	Yes	No
1	2	3	4	5	Burger	6.50	Yes	No
1	2	3	4	5	C&S Sandwich	6.95	Yes	No
1	2	3	4	5	Calamari	8.95	Yes	No
1	2	3	4	5	Curry	10.95	Yes	No
1	2	3	4	5	Fish & Chips	7.95	Yes	No
1	2	3	4	5	Mare	10.50	Yes	No
1	2	3	4	5	Marinara	8.95	Yes	No
1	2	3	4	5	Pasta Roll	10.50	Yes	No

What other items should be added to the menu?

_____

_____

_____

_____

What items should be taken off the menu?

_____

_____

_____

_____

Thank you.

The menu is the nucleus of the restaurant's retail activity. It is the purest expression of the operator's marketing plan and management's blueprint for profitability. It's also a map to optimum performance for the kitchen and dining room staff. Here's an example of value-perception pricing at work.

Using the old method, the chef or kitchen manager would introduce the daily specials during the pre-shift briefing like this: "Tonight we are featuring the fresh Pacific Lingcod. This is a 7-oz. fillet, broiled medium rare, and served with Georgia pecan chutney and pan-roasted potatoes, for $12.95."

In other words, here it is, sell it. And 99% of the time, the item was priced using formula pricing—taking the raw cost and applying a preset multiplier. Chances are there was little creative thought put into the pricing, no consideration for special merchandising information, such as pecan chutney made from scratch in the kitchen, or lingcod line-caught locally.

These are the special points of interest and excitement that create value for the restaurant guest. When they are sitting at the table with menu open, the waiter or waitress has the opportunity to create special interest about the food.

In the new method, we would encourage the chef or kitchen manager to prepare a sample of each special, and allow the waiters and waitresses to taste test it.

Ask the waitstaff "How much do you think we can charge for it?" Instantaneously, the food server's brain engages, and each begins to analyze what price is appropriate and consistent with guest expectations. Remarkably, waiters and waitresses will frequently suggest a selling price that is higher than the kitchen's recommendation. The Pacific Lingcod, priced at $12.95 by the chef could be priced at $13.95 by the servers.

Servers intuitive sense of pricing is highly consistent with what the guest will pay. And don't worry about setting price points too high based on server feedback. Servers are always reluctant to sell overpriced menu items—it directly impacts their tips!

Waiters and waitresses must become ambassadors for the menu, particularly the specials. Specials are unique preparations with inherently high-profit margins. The food server who has tasted the specials can now appreciate the flavor, appearance, and texture characteristics firsthand. This allows the them to offer suggestions based upon firsthand experience. The idea is to avoid the following scene—one which is played out in restaurants more often than we might like to believe:

A restaurant guest asks the waitress for a recommendation about which of the restaurant's menu items are particularly good. The waitress, who has not had the opportunity to taste the menu items, responds without thinking: "I don't know, I can't afford to eat here!"

This isn't what operators want to hear from their sales ambassadors. The point is obvious. Consider a very different scenario when the waitress is asked for a recommendation, and says: "I recommend the broiled free-range chicken. I sampled it myself this evening. It's tender, flavorful, low-in-fat and accompanied by spicy, grilled baby potatoes. A fantastic meal!"

The result? The free-range chicken will be one of the first specials to sell out. Get the serving team involved in experiencing the food, and the sales of specials will go off the chart!

The real power of the value-perception pricing strategy is that it opens up the window of opportunity for windfall profits. It also causes the operator to examine the gross profit contributions of each menu item. It helps to establish a clear, understandable blueprint for profitability. This must be the DSR's new calling as a profitability consultant. Forget selling products. Start selling solutions. Build credibility.

COLD CALLING

Cold calling is one of the greatest, if not the most important skill to be learned in sales. It's the foundation for a successful career in selling. You must show yourself to be one who knows the customer's business. You must be prepared to consult, and to present profitable solutions to the customer's problems.

I'm often asked to offer tips to distributor sales reps about how to effectively "cold call" a potential customer— particularly one who has been wedded to a competitor for years. How do you get his or her attention while still maintaining a professional and high-profile image?

First, you must think like a consultant and earn the opportunity to make your presentation. You have to develop the credibility associated with value-driven thinking. The payoff for this work is simple: the operator will gain a more favorable gross margin, guests will receive greater value from the menu items they buy, and you will increase account penetration. In other words, you create a WIN-WIN-WIN situation.

A cold-call presentation must be carefully scripted in advance so that the benefits you offer are clearly perceived by the operator within the first minute of your presentation.

Today's operator, manager, or chain executive has less time, less patience, and less interest in the input of others into daily business decisions. Salespeople are a necessary distraction in a day typically characterized by 50 mini-meetings and more than 100 interruptions. But believe it or not, once you demonstrate that you can help solve problems, streamline purchasing, coordinate menu planning, provide recipe costing, and deliver measurable profits—without increasing costs—you will be a welcome sight whenever you call on that account. The very qualities in operators that make them so tough and so resistant to cold calls can actually work in your favor over the long run.

Capture the attention of a potential customer by offering an operating tip, menu-design concept, or management technique that will deliver immediate gratification. This will differentiate you from your competitors. Your future customers will see you in an entirely different light—not just as another ordertaker, but as a consultant, with knowledge, experience, and information crucial to their success. Doing this correctly is no small order. It requires lots of thinking, planning, research, and attention to a wide range of details.

Offering solutions and suggestions will open the door, from there you can build sales volume directly by helping to solve your customers' problems. This is truly consultative selling. It will inevitably result in an account relationship based on the value-added benefits that you have in your tool kit, and not on your willingness to lower prices on the products you sell.

Here is a great menu-pricing concept that will immediately capture the attention of your prospective new customer:

In the first three seconds, once your prospective customer has leaned back in his chair, crossed his arms, and given you the floor, ask, "How many orders of Dungeness Crab Cakes did you sell last year?" Once you have the answer, write it down on a pad of paper, and present the following "killer" idea I call the rounding strategy. It is the very definition of the "value-perception" pricing discipline. This concept is incredibly simple, and will always produce interest, if not "hook 'em" right on the spot. Notice the Dungeness Crab Cakes in Figure 19 that are selling for $14.60. In this menu-item listing, all the prices end in either: $0.40, $0.60, $0.75 or $0.95. This is usually the result of formula pricing, discussed in Chapter 10.

FIGURE 19

THE WRONG APPROACH TO MENU PRICING

JOE'S SPECIALS

DUNGENESS CRAB CAKES	
A Northwest Version of a Traditional Favorite	14.60
OREGON STARRY FLOUNDER PARMESAN	
With Fresh Lemon, Crispy Capers and Beurre Blanc	12.75
FRANK'S ETOUFEE	
With Rock Shrimp, Crawfish and Chicken	15.60
CANADIAN RED ROCKFISH	
Seared with Dungeoness Crab and Sherry	13.40
ALASKAN TROLL KING SALMON	
Roasted on a Cedar Plank	19.95
HALIBUT FISH & CHIPS	
Beer Battered Halibut with French Fries and Cole Slaw	9.95
NORTHWEST MIXED GRILL	
With Dungeoness Crabcake, Salmon & Ling Cod	17.95
OCEAN SCALLOP SAUTE	
With Mushrooms, Artichoke Hearts, Tomato & Bacon	15.75

Consumers only acknowledge certain price points when they read menus. For menu items priced over $5, the guest only recognizes price increments of .50¢ and .95¢. In other words, the guest doesn't register any difference between $14.60 to $14.95.

For menu items priced under $5, the issue is less clear. At lower price points, the significance of a dime or a quarter is much greater. As a general rule, menu items with price points set at even 25¢ increments seem to be agreeable to most consumers. If the operator can charge $3.15 for sausage and eggs, he can probably charge $3.25 without any resistance from the customer.

Here's your cold call opportunity. You can show an operator how to immediately increase his flow-through profits. Imagine yourself pointing to the menu and indicating one menu item that is priced using formula pricing. Let's use the Dungeness Crab Cakes selling at $14.60. The operator tells you that on a typical day 25 orders of the Dungeness Crab Cakes are sold. This 25-per-day volume multiplied by 365 days equals 9,125 sold annually. Explain that by applying the rounding strategy they can charge $14.95 instead of the current price of $14.60 without decreasing sales.

You are handing your prospective customer a gift. In effect you've shown this operator how to create $3,193.75 in flow-through profit. You've also given him a very good reason to do business with you instead of the competition. You've taken the first step toward building a relationship with a new customer.

This powerful, yet simple theory first occurred to me many years ago during a to visit a prominent Los Angeles dinner house—one known for prime rib. The restaurant had over $4 million in annual sales—a big volume in the mid-'80s. They also had a reputation for being one of the true innovators in our business. When I opened the menu I noticed their house specialty—Prime Rib, selling for $14.05. I did a double take. Did I read the price correctly? Were they really charging $14.05?

Curious, I summoned the waiter who in turn called the general manager of the unit. After some preliminary chitchat, I introduced myself as a fellow operator and asked about the $14.05 price point on the prime rib. What was the strategic thinking behind that nickel? Since this was a well known and highly respected Los Angeles "institution," I had visions of a corporate boardroom with all the seats filled. The corporate chef, directors of marketing, operations, finance, real estate, development were all considering, in painful detail, the various price points that might be appropriate for a high-profile signature item such as the full-cut prime rib.

Was this a case of high-level, proprietary and secretive thinking? Could the price point have been set as a result of a carefully analyzed and systematized process of formulating prices? Well, not exactly.

The GM summoned the executive chef who was also on duty. The next thing I knew, the executive chef was standing at tableside, trusty clipboard in hand, thrilled to have the opportunity to explain the company's price-setting discipline. He ran his fingers through various sheets on the clipboard until he located the full-cut prime rib, studied the figures with great concentration, and after a pause, he explained.

"We calculate the raw cost of the entire prime-rib dinner, down to the penny, including side salad, garnish, baked potato, even the sprig of parsley." He seemed very proud of the figures he was showing me. "As you can see, the total cost of the prime rib is $4.82. Then we apply a standardized multiplier to establish a retail selling price. In this case the markup yielded a selling price of $14.02."

At this point there was an uncomfortable silence for a second or two. Then the chef added, "I went ahead and made the decision to round the price up to $14.05."

He looked to his General Manager for approval. The GM nodded absently. I asked how many orders of prime rib they sold in a year, to which they answered about 10,000.

"Did you realize," I asked, "that your guests wouldn't perceive a difference between $14.05 and $14.50? Why not capture the extra profit that would come from pricing the prime rib at $14.50 if their perception is the same?"

The General Manager fixed an intent stare on me, as if he had just been blinded by a flash of the obvious. I could see him doing the math, multiplying those 10,000 orders of prime rib by the extra 45¢. An extra $4,500 in profit. I think he even figured out his share of the profit in his bonus plan! He smiled and said to me, "Now that's a fantastic concept!"

But this is no concept. It is simple common sense. Pricing menu items according to their perceived value is done daily in the restaurant business. This experience had a decided impact on my thinking about value-perception pricing and the importance of positioning yourself as a consultant with a solid, fundamental pricing philosophy. Once you help an operator grasp the significance of this pricing philosophy, you have also helped their profit potential increase by at least 2–3%. You will find your customers showing significant interest in your knowledge as a consultative salesperson, and your success in integrating your own products into their menu will only be a matter of time.

CHAPTER 12

INTRODUCTION TO THE
GROSS PROFIT PHILOSOPHY

The true measure of profitability of any menu item can be determined by examining its actual gross profit, or profit margin, as in the spreadsheet in Figure 20. By knowing which menu items have the most favorable gross profit margins, you have the data needed to help your customer decide which items to aggressively merchandise, promote, and sell—and which ones you don't want to emphasize.

FIGURE 20

GROSS PROFIT SPREADSHEET (PARTIAL) GROSS PROFIT CONTRIBUTION								
LUNCH THEORETICAL	Menu Price	Item Cost	Gross Profit	No. Sold	% Sold	Total $ Sold	Total $ Cost	Cost %
Shrimp Louie	11.95	2.56	9.39	5	0.29	59.75	12.80	21.42
Crab Louie	12.95	4.15	8.80	8	0.46	103.60	33.20	32.05
Spinach Salad	7.50	2.15	5.35	2	0.12	15.00	4.30	28.67
Quiche	6.50	1.52	4.98	32	1.84	208.00	48.64	23.38
Pasta Primavera	5.50	2.35	3.15	8	0.46	44.00	18.80	42.73

Consider the impact of this thinking as it might apply to an example I described earlier. If 150,000 guests open a menu each year, your customer has 150,000 opportunities to sell them a menu item with an additional 10¢ in profit. 150,000 dimes equals $15,000 in new profit.

FIGURE 21

GROSS PROFIT COMPARISON

LUNCH THEORETICAL	Menu Price	Item Cost	Gross Profit	Cost %
Chocolate Amaretto Pie	3.95	0.54	3.41	14%
ChocolateMousse Pie	3.95	0.49	3.46	12%
Fresh Strawberries	3.95	1.25	2.70	32%
Mississippi Mud Pie	3.95	1.26	2.69	32%
New York Cheesecake	3.95	1.52	2.43	38%
ChocolateCream Pie	2.95	0.69	2.26	23%
Chocolate Crêpe	2.95	0.51	2.44	17%
Pumpkin Pie	2.75	0.31	2.44	11%
Lemon Tart	2.50	0.25	2.25	10%
Ice Cream	1.25	0.21	1.04	17%

Consider another example. Note the difference between the gross profit of the chocolate amaretto cream pie and the New York-style cheesecake in Figure 21. Both desserts offer identical price points, but the chocolate amaretto cream pie offers a 98¢ greater gross profit contribution. Therefore, when merchandising desserts, the operator's focus should be on selling the chocolate amaretto cream pie. During the pre-shift briefing, the waitstaff should be encouraged to promote the chocolate amaretto cream pie over the New York-style cheesecake. This promotion should be further reinforced throughout the shift. If 25% of the orders for the cheesecake can be shifted to the chocolate amaretto pie, the result is an added profit of over $1,200 per year— for one dessert item! (See Figure 22.)

FIGURE 22

COMPARISON MARGIN SELLING

New York Cheesecake 5,000 orders sold

Chocolate Amaretto Pie 6,000 orders sold

Gross Profit Advantage of Chocolate Amaretto Pie

98¢ per slice

A shift of 25% of 5,000 cheesecake orders = 1,250 orders

If 25% of New York Cheese cake sales are shifted
to Chocolate Amaretto Pie...

ADDITIONAL ANNUAL PROFIT: $1,225

While the execution of this principle is fairly simple, operators must learn, with your help, how to correctly calculate gross profit contribution using recipe costing and value-perception pricing. Then, you must teach them how to integrate this new thinking into their day-to-day operations. Becoming more profitable is an achievable goal—if they work with you as their primary menu expert.

As a consultant, you have to deliver a clear and strong call to action. You must challenge and help reshape the pattern of your customer's business thinking. Although you are serving to enlighten your customers, it can sometimes be intimidating to them. So, go slow and do your homework. Understand how to implement the points I'm explaining, and follow through until this philosophy becomes an integral part of every aspect of your customer's operation. While some operators may embrace this thinking right away, others may require months or even a year for it to settle in.

All of the principles that affect menu decisions—recipe costing, percentage target myopia, value-perception pricing, the gross profit philosophy—are fundamental menu concepts, which align the highest profit menu items with the purchasing predisposition of restaurant patrons. Regardless of all the sophisticated menu textbooks that have been written, and all of the computerized menu-design software that has been developed, this is selling by going back to basics. It's a matter of repeatedly reinforcing simple, time-tested principles and disciplines. It means offering your customers a stable, consistent, and logical menu-development philosophy. Your ideas should be gratefully received, because in the highly complicated world of foodservice, everyone in the operating community is interested in revisiting the fundamentals: to clarify, organize, and focus their thinking around a proven set of core menu principles.

CHAPTER 13

Menu Layout And Design

How can you help your customers create the perfect menu? What are the design principles, layout and graphic techniques, styles, and color concepts that can showcase those items that are inherently more profitable?

The answer is a process called "menu engineering." It is based on the creative use of highlighting and layout-design techniques to subtly influence diners' selection behaviors. The purpose of menu engineering is to sell those menu items and specials that offer the greatest value and, at the same time, generate the most favorable gross profit contribution.

In the early stages of your menu-consulting activities, you should be prepared to spend many hours studying menu layouts and design—the elements that mold and shape a menu's profit power to perfection. The process starts by examining the ways in which operators have traditionally presented their menus.

MENU PRESENTATION FORMAT

Let's start at the very beginning—when the patron is first handed the menu. The conventional wisdom has been, "Keep your menus sharp, crisp, and bright." A clean menu indicates a clean restaurant. A clean restaurant reflects positively on the operator's sense of pride in his facility and on the attractiveness of the food and beverages served.

For decades, restaurant operators have used laminated menus as the format-of-choice. This approach has been viewed as the most effective and economical way to keep menus clean and resistant to folds, tears, and other visible signs of wear.

Laminated menus are expensive. A typical two-page, 11 1/2" X 14" version can easily cost $5 or more, but the benefit is that the laminated menu will last for three months or more before needing to be replaced. In addition, the high front-end cost may be offset to some degree by volume purchasing, significantly reducing the cost of each menu.

The era of the laminated menu, however, has past. One reason is that this format fails miserably in accommodating the most important feature of a successful menu: flexibility. Today's foodservice competition is fierce. Every chain and independent restaurant needs to respond quickly to changes in consumer tastes, and take advantage of shifting market trends. Constant variations in the supply and price of raw food products further complicate the equation, placing additional pressure on menu managers who try to offer new and different core menu items, as well as daily or weekly specials.

Also significant is the growing importance of applying creativity, imagination and innovation to the development of new menu items. Everyone is madly searching for the newest food, spice or garnish that can attract new guests and keep existing ones coming back.

The plastic menu jacket made its entry onto the foodservice industry scene in the mid-'80s. This format offered a perfect solution to the need for menu flexibility. Featuring a clear sleeve for printed inserts, the plastic jacket is available in a wide variety of sizes, shapes and styles to complement a wide range of full-service operations. Best of all, it is low in cost—roughly half the price of the conventional laminated menu.

Operators are now able to use the services of the quick-print shops. The paper insert "shells" can be printed in volume, making colored borders and headings affordable. The operator can use a laser printer to add current menu items, adjust prices, or delete slow movers. They can produce a high-quality, visually appealing menu, with all of the aesthetic advantages they had with laminated menus.

Why don't all operators embrace this superior method of menu presentation? There are a number of reasons. The first is laziness. Once a huge order of laminated menus has been received, no more thinking is required. Second, the durability of the laminated menu is still a benefit. Third, many operators can't face the reality of throwing away cases of unused (although outdated) menus. Finally, there is a false perception that there is cost savings in using the laminated menu.

In the final analysis, successful operators should have a menu jacket that is fresh, timely, exciting, and in tune with the changing preferences of the consumer. The menu must reflect the excitement, quality, and tone of the dining experience. The menu jacket is an important first step in creating a menu that is consistent with the image the establishment presents to the public. If you don't sell menu covers, you should consider it. At least make sure you are knowledgeable about menu-cover manufacturers. Ask them to send sample menu kits to your accounts. As a consultant, you are facilitating the process of change, helping your customers through an important transition toward increased profitability.

DESKTOP PUBLISHING

You have demonstrated the value of using menus that can change quickly and to adapt to shifts in consumer tastes, and the trends that seem to emerge overnight.

Delivering an attractive menu will depend largely on the magic of desktop publishing. The quick-printing capability of a desktop system, whether in-house or through a local copy center, can give your customer's menu a thoroughly professional look at half the cost of a traditional printer. This desktop advantage also allows for the affordable printing of colorful headings, borders, graphics, and other design items. Brightly printed menu pages accented with color and graphics are essential features of a successful menu created to drive profitability.

There are many user-friendly software programs on the market, both for menu design and graphic design. You and your customer can quickly become comfortable with the process of desktop menu design, again, allowing you to increase a price, delete a slow seller, or add a new item with great convenience, and respond quickly to changing consumer preferences.

PAGE POSITIONING

People don't read menus from front to back and top to bottom. Studies show that as a guest scans a menu, their eyes follow a predictable pattern. Using this pattern to an operator's advantage is called page positioning. I was first introduced to the concept by nationally-recognized foodservice management teacher and consultant, Tom Costello. Whether a menu uses a three-, two-, or single-panel configuration, the patron's eyes flow across the page following a predictable "path," subconsciously searching for points of visual interest (see Figure 23).

FIGURE 23

EYE-GAZE PATTERNS

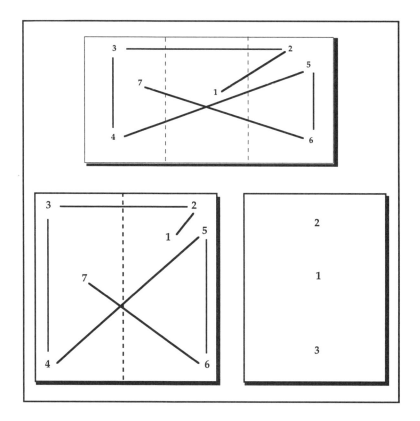

As a profitability consultant, you now have an opportunity to help them make their menus more efficient. Take advantage of the way diners peruse a menu, and establish yourself as a knowledgeable menu expert. Ask your customers if they know whether their menu items offering the most favorable gross profit are in the path of a patron's eye-gaze pattern.

FIGURE 24

A FIELD-FORMATTED MENU

Scallops Sausalito
Tender scallops sauteed in white wine, garlic, mushrooms, and green onions, simmered in a rich Bechamel sauce. Served with rice. $12.95

Crabtown Chicken
A tender whole chicken breast stuffed with crab and garlic butter, then baked and topped with a sherry cream sauce. $13.95

Prawns Saute
Plump and tender prawns, delicately sauteed with mushrooms, garlic, sherry and lemon. Served with rice and fresh vegetables. $12.50

Baked Avocado and Shrimp Diablo
Two garden fresh avocado halves, brimming with a mixture of bay shrimp, water chestnuts and green onions, topped with a rich Mornay sauce, sprinkled with fresh grated Swiss and Parmesan cheeses, and baked on a bed of rice. $9.95

Smoked Salmon Fettuccine
Delicious flakes of smoked salmon combined with "al dente" fettuccine noodles, cream, and fresh grated parmesan cheese. $13.95

Fisherman's Net
Crab, shrimp, baby clams and scallops combined with "al dente" fettuccine noodles, cream and fresh grated parmesan cheese. $14.95

As you examine your customer's menu, remember that not all menu formats are structured to benefit from eye-gaze patterns. Those menus that present items in a field format (Figure 24) will apply and can be improved. However, menus that present items vertically, in the form of a category listing (Figure 25), will generally not respond to eye-gaze patterns.

FIGURE 25

A CATEGORY-FORMATTED MENU

LUNCH SALADS

With oven baked bread and choice of homemade dressings: Honey Dijon Mustard, Peppercorn Ranch, Thousand Island, or Blue Cheese.

CHICKEN CAESAR...$6.95
Crisp romaine lettuce, croutons, Caesar dressing, and grated Parmesan, topped with grilled strips of chicken.

LE CLUB SALAD...$6.75
Crisp salad greens, shaved turkey, shaved ham, diced bacon, chopped eggs, cheese, tomatoes, and croutons.

TOMATO VINAIGRETTE PASTA SALAD.....................$5.95
Crisp salad greens topped with pasta salad. Served with tomatoes, and Sassy Apples.

SOUP AND SALAD...$5.95
Your choice of homemade soup and one of these great "mini" salads: The House, Chicken Caesar, or Le Club Salad.

TEXAS STUFFERS

Hand selected #1 potatoes stuffed with flavor. All the way means butter, bacon, cheese, sour cream, and chives.

SOUTHWESTERN...$4.95
Monterey Jack cheese, bacon, and butter, topped with avocado slices, sour cream, and chives.

VEGETABLE STUFFER...$4.50
Fresh vegetables and Hollandaise sauce.

CHEYENNE STUFFER...$4.50
Topped with chorizo, cheese, and hot salsa.

FIGURE 26

SHOWCASING THE SPECIALS: WORD OFFSET HIGHLIGHTING

WHITE WINES

For greater ease in selection,
our white wines are listed in order of dryness to sweetness.

Sauvignon Blanc
Dry, medium bodied with a subtle, smokey flavor   Obeste $13.95

Chardonnay
Rich flavor, crisp and dry—an award winner   San Martin $12.95

French Colombard
Crisp and dry—best in its class   Parducci $10.95

White Zinfandel
Medium dry and fruity, from the San Benito Mountains   Enz $11.95

Special

Pinot Noir Blanc "Eye of the Swan"
This highly unusual wine features a unique copper cast in
the same shade as the eyes of a black swan in vintner
August Sebastiani's aviary. Full bodied, dry, with a fruity
nose. A unique white wine made from red Pinot Noir grapes. $11.95

Grey Riesling
A full-bodied, dry white wine, full of tradition   Wente $10.95

Gewurztraminer
From the St. Inez Valley. Spicy and rich   Firestone $12.95

Chenin Blanc
Tart and fruity, yet with a soft bouquet   Mirassou $12.95

Special

White Riesling
From an award winning winery in the Santa Cruz Mountains
comes this delicatley sweet, flavorful and spicy Riesling.
A limited bottling, subject to availability. $12.95

WORD OFFSET HIGHLIGHTING

Remember, people only peruse a menu, and their eyes scan the page in a predictable path. The reader's gaze is easily attracted to any pattern change or deviation. For example, consider the placement of the word "Special" to the immediate left of the wine selection shown in Figure 26. Now, the word "Special" is not the key to this technique. The word used could be "new" or "traditional" or any of a multitude of descriptive words that could accent a menu item. The key is that the word is placed asymmetrically—at a slight angle— and therefore catches the eye. Invariably, this will lead to an increase in the selection rate of any similarly targeted item by as much as 10–20%.

If you've already focused your client's attention on the importance of the gross profit contributions of various menu items, you can now assist them by simply placing the word "Special," or any other descriptive word next to certain items with a high gross profit contribution. Your customer can immediately increase the sale of these items significantly! How many incremental gross profit dollars can you influence in this way over the course of a year?

THE "BOXING" TECHNIQUE

There is no menu engineering tool that is more powerful than the "boxing" technique. Look at Figures 27 and 28, which illustrate before and after versions of the boxing effect. By simply drawing a box around a high profit item, an operator can focus the guest's attention. Generally speaking, guest selection of an item or group of items that has been boxed can be expected to increase by approximately 15%. Let's take a look at how this can impact your customer's annual profit.

FIGURE 27

MENU BEFORE BOXING

Pa likes his chicken fried ...

Pop believes there's no chicken better than southern fried. Cooked golden crisp and seasoned with special spices to pull out the natural chicken flavors.

Chicken Deluxe $7.95
Fresh parts from a whole chicken (that's eight pieces). Choice of any two veggies, plus a corn muffin.

Chicken Dinner $4.50
Two parts from one of our fresh chickens, cooked perfectly, with your choice of two veggies and a corn muffin.

Leo's Chicken Livers $5.50
A pound of selected, lightly breaded livers, tender and delicious, with any two veggies and a corn muffin.

... Ma likes hers broiled.

Mom says broiled is better. We must agree, because Mom knows her chicken. Honey dipped, then charbroiled but still as juicy as you can get.

Charbroiled Henhouse Chicken $7.50
Whole fresh chicken, charbroiled until crisp along with your choice of any two veggies and a corn muffin.

Charbroiled Half Chicken $4.50
The same fresh chicken, only a smaller portion, charbroiled to taste with your choice of two veggies and a corn muffin.

Backyard Barbecued Chicken $5.95
Our own sweet barbecue sauce makes this breast of chicken really special. Served with two veggies and a biscuit.

FIGURE 28

MENU AFTER BOXING

Pa likes his chicken fried ...

Pop believes there's no chicken better than southern fried. Cooked golden crisp and seasoned with special spices to pull out the natural chicken flavors.

Chicken Deluxe $7.95
Fresh parts from a whole chicken (that's eight pieces). Choice of any two veggies, plus a corn muffin.

Chicken Dinner $4.50
Two parts from one of our fresh chickens, cooked perfectly, with your choice of two veggies and a corn muffin.

Leo's Chicken Livers $5.50
A pound of selected, lightly breaded livers, tender and delicious, with any two veggies and a corn muffin.

... Ma likes hers broiled.

Mom says broiled is better. We must agree, because Mom knows her chicken. Honey dipped, then charbroiled but still as juicy as you can get.

Charbroiled Henhouse Chicken $7.50
Whole fresh chicken, charbroiled until crisp along with your choice of any two veggies and a corn muffin.

Charbroiled Half Chicken $4.50
The same fresh chicken, only a smaller portion, charbroiled to taste with your choice of two veggies and a corn muffin.

Backyard Barbecued Chicken $5.95
Our own sweet barbecue sauce makes this breast of chicken really special. Served with two veggies and a biscuit.

Figure 29 shows five menu items. Assume that each of these items is served 10 times a day, for a total of 50 covers. The Shrimp Louie has a gross profit of $9.39. This is considerably higher than the gross profit of the other menu items, whose average gross profit is $7.24.

By applying boxing to the Shrimp Louie, we can increase its sales from 20% of the menu mix to 30%, an increase of five additional sales per day. Five sales X $1.72 additional gross profit per sale = $8.60/day in extra flow-through profit. This comes to $3,139/year. Is there any doubt that this action could get the attention of your customer and instantly build your credibility?

FIGURE 29

HIGHLIGHTING THE PROFIT GENERATOR

GROSS PROFIT COMPARISON			
ITEM	RETAIL	COST	GROSS PROFIT
Shrimp Louie	11.95	2.56	9.39
Crab Louie	12.95	4.15	8.80
Shrimp Sandwich	9.50	2.07	7.43
Crab Sandwich	10.95	3.57	7.38
Spinach Salad	7.50	2.15	5.35

A note: When recommending the boxing effect, you should caution the customer to avoid using it too frequently. Usually, two boxed items is the maximum that should be used on each page of a menu (see Figure 28).

THE SHADING EFFECT

Shading is another menu engineering technique that can be used to increase sales of high gross profit items. Menu items that are accented by the use of the shading usually show an increase in selection rate of at least 10%.

Figure 30 shows an example of the shading technique. Notice how the vegetable minestrone is located inside of a shaded box which is offset by a dark shadow on the bottom and right sides. This shadow creates a three-dimensional effect, and the item seems to lift off the page. This causes a disruption in the customer's eye-gaze pattern and the eyes stop briefly, just long enough for the mind to consider the vegetable minestrone selection. Again, since people don't really read menus, any item that attracts the eye has an higher chance of being selected.

FIGURE 30

SHADING THE MENU

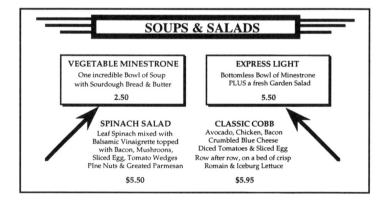

SHOWCASING

This approach is a more artistic extension of the boxing technique used to lead the guest to a particular menu category. It may even be employed to highlight a particular merchandising strategy. For example, in Figure 31, fresh fish is being showcased as a welcome alternative on a steakhouse menu.

Showcasing identifies the individual item, food group, or menu section being highlighted by featuring a unique border, special graphic treatment, or highly visible pattern or "irregularity." Like boxing and shading, these techniques are used to attract the eye and project the feeling that something special is happening. Remember, readers' eyes are bored as they sweep across the page. They are seeking relief and interest, elements out of the ordinary. Don't be surprised if sales of items showcased on your menu enjoy immediate sales increases of 20% or more.

FIGURE 31

MENU SHOWCASING

FRESH FISH

At Randell's we apply the highest standards to guarantee the freshest fish available in Greenville. All seafood is carefully inspected upon arrival to ensure quality and freshness.

Lunch Cut $ 8.50
Dinner Cut $13.95

New York Steak
A generous 14 oz. cut of perfectly
aged NY steak, broiled to order.... $13.95

Beef Back Ribs
Thick, meaty ribs, slow cooked and
glazed with our tangy BBQ sauce.... $10.95

T-Bone Steak
Juicy and flavorful, a 25 oz. bone-in
cut that covers the plate.... $14.95

Filet Mignon
A 12 oz. cut of the finest aged
beef tenderloin.... $15.95
A 7 oz. petite cut.... $12.95

FIGURE 32

PERSONALIZING THE MENU

Calamari Steak & Fries $8.95

A lightly breaded calamari steak pan fried with
garlic lemon butter served with french fries.

 ## Nantucket Mixed Grill $19.95

Maryland Crab Cakes, local fresh Cod, and jumbo
Scallops flavored with genuine "Old Bay" seasonings.
Served with Martha's Vineyard Corn Pudding.

Maryland Crab Cakes $15.95

Not exactly Cape Cod, but close. An Atlantic-style
preparation featuring "Old Bay" seasoningsa and
succulent Pacific Dungeness Crab, pan-fried and
served with fries and apple cider coleslaw.

Boston-Style Cod Duglere $14.95

Fresh local Lingcod, pan-seared to lock in the full
flavor. Topped with a New England combination of
tomato, dill, mushrooms, and parsley.

SIGNATURE ICONS

This technique is the most direct of the menu-engineering techniques you might introduce to your customer. It's also the most fun and the most effective. The idea is to help your customers create a miniaturized version of their logo or similar graphic (see Figure 32) that can create a visual connection to their restaurant's personality or distinctive style. Representations of the restaurant's name, location, type of service, or decor offer possibilities for a signature icon. You may also gain ideas from the type of food served, such as using a miniature Italian flag for an Italian concept or a pineapple on a Hawaiian menu. In my former seafood restaurant, we used a little seagull.

The signature icon should be placed slightly to the left of the menu item, creating an interesting diversion for the eye The icon subtly suggests that the item is of the "signature" variety. The restaurant patron will assume that since management wants to place extra emphasis and attention on this item, it must be special! Signature icons also add style, flair, and character to a menu, while serving as an excellent tool to shift the diner's attention to more profitable menu items.

Let me describe some simple applications. All menus have certain items that can't be removed, because of consistent customer demand, regardless of seasonal availability or cost factors. For example, removing a green salad from the menu is not an option, even though during certain times of the year lettuce is extremely expensive. Operators can't stop serving salad when lettuce becomes expensive. They can't say to their guests, "Sorry, the price of lettuce is sky high right now and we can't make any money on salads, so how about a bowl of clam chowder?" Instead, they must simply absorb the extra cost and wait for lettuce prices to fall.

This is where the signature icon can become extremely useful. Assume that it's winter, and that the price of lettuce is 40% more now than during the summer months. Move the signature icon away from the Caesar salad, which is popular and profitable in the summer and fall, and place it next to the French onion soup. This item has a cost that remains relatively stable throughout the year, and is more profitable than the Caesar salad during the winter.

Let's do the math...

Assume that during the summer months, both the Caesar salad and the French Onion Soup have a raw cost of $1 each. During the winter months, however, the raw cost of the Caesar salad goes up to $1.25.

On average, your customer sells 50 Caesar salads per day, winter or summer. By placing a signature icon next to the French onion soup during the winter when lettuce prices are high, the operator can shift as many as 40% of the guests' selections away from the Caesar salad and over to the French onion soup. That's 20 redirected purchases per day, or 2,400 purchases for a 4-month period. Each month your customer will make $600 in pure profit you've helped create by making this simple menu adjustment. And that's on just one item!

Beginning to get the picture? It's relatively easy to make a significant profit impact with virtually any of the menu-engineering techniques. All of these techniques—word highlighting, boxing, shading, showcasing, and signature icons, represent variations on a basic theme: create pattern-breakers on the menu, devices that are subtle yet stylish, eye-catching and image-building for any foodservice operation. Besides being very profitable, the items highlighted by these menu engineering techniques must be great food items with excellent appeal in their own right. It's important to include an attractive plate presentation, lots of color, ample portions, and interesting names and descriptions.

CATEGORICAL MENU ITEM PLACEMENT

If your customers are resistant to altering the look of their menu by applying menu engineering techniques, all hope is not lost. You still have a secret weapon: menu item placement.

Another subconscious reading pattern is to resist reading vertically, studying each successive line and menu item. As a result, the most frequently selected items from a menu category are those listed in first and last position, because these are the easiest and simplest for the reader to find and focus on. Therefore, those items should be the items with the highest gross profit (see Figure 33). The items placed in the middle of a category will be the least selected, and therefore, should feature the lowest gross profit contribution. It's as simple as that.

FIGURE 33

MENU ITEM PLACEMENT

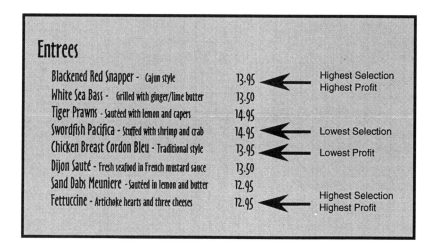

Here is another opportunity for you to help your customer easily increase profits through menu engineering. The first step is to study the menu to determine if it is laid out in categories, such as appetizers, entrées, soups and salads, seafood, poultry, side dishes, desserts, and beverages. Look for categories that have at least 6–8 menu items. This is the size and scale that works best in demonstrating the magic of proper menu item placement.

Next, determine the gross profit contributions of each of the items in a category. Make sure the first menu item listed has the highest gross profit contribution. The last item listed should have the second highest gross profit contribution. Does the balance of the menu selections reflect a progressively smaller and less attractive gross profit contribution? All it takes is a simple reordering of each category to increase the sales of the more profitable items on the menu.

Menu item placement offers another significant advantage from a selling perspective. Your customers rarely have the exact menu costing and recipe explosion information necessary to calculate gross profit contributions for each menu item in the first place. This represents a terrific opportunity for you to cost the recipes and return to the operator with a revised menu-item placement order. And you can provide them with examples of how profitable these simple changes can be.

Because menu engineering techniques are so simple and so profitable, many operators are tempted to load their menu with icons, shading, boxes and words going in every direction. Caution them to be prudent, however. Limit the use of these treatments to no more than one menu item in ten. A well-designed menu may feature one of each of these applications, subtly woven into the menu's body, and success in subverting and redirecting selection behaviors is based upon choosing menu items with the most favorable gross profit contribution.

Be mindful, too, that these techniques should work on the patron's subconscious mind. A restaurant guest never knows that a well-designed menu has been engineered. In many surveys and guest intercepts, people who ordered menu items that were highlighted, were asked if they noticed an icon accenting certain items on the menu. In 99% of the cases, they did not! Capitalize on the tendency of today's guest to scan rather than read. Position menu items strategically to increase sales and profit potential.

Each of these menu engineering techniques will provide you with tremendous leverage in breaking the ice during cold calls. They can also help you achieve account penetration goals with your existing customers. These techniques underscore the fundamental concept that your customer's profitability can be easily improved. All it takes is understanding the power of menu engineering, and value-perception-based and gross-profit-driven pricing. You hold the key to this understanding.

Be careful of how you share this valuable knowledge and insight. Leverage it to the fullest with your customers to keep them coming back for more. Foster a sense of dependency on you as their primary foodservice consultant and the DSR to whom they pledge the lion's share of their business.

CHAPTER 14

THREE TRENDS IN MENU DEVELOPMENT AND EVOLUTION

As a menu and profitability consultant, you will be expected to keep up on the current trends in every foodservice market segment. Just as women's hem lines change from year to year, so do eating preferences. This causes operators to constantly make changes on their menus to reflect the consumer's never-ending search for freshness, excitement, variety, and novelty. Major changes in dining preferences are always taking shape. Different strategies associated with menu development will become popular, fade away, and then return with new strength.

SIDE DISHES SELL

In the early days, à la carte side dishes were a standard around which menus were developed. They helped restaurant guests build a meal to their satisfaction, based on taste, budget, and time available for dining. In recent years, side dishes have reappeared in response to the craze we now call "grazing." Food lovers and gourmets build a meal around smaller portions. This allows enjoyment of a wide variety of flavors and textures.

Because of the growing diversity of foods available, side dishes take on a strategic new significance. As costs continue to increase for the operator, the pressure to raise prices is enormous. However, increased competition in the marketplace, comparable values in take-out and delivery, and the instability of discretionary income make raising prices a risky proposition.

Side-dishes, however, offer the opportunity to create an up-sell situation that can add anywhere from $1.50 to $3.50 to the check average. While starches, vegetables, and other appetizing goodies used to be considered simply "plate fillers," they can now be merchandised as sexy and zesty "must-try" dishes.

Entrée prices, which drive menu value perceptions, can be kept low while selling one or more side dishes to bring the average check back up to a level that can produce a satisfactory gross profit contribution. The subtlety of this technique must be understood and appreciated by your client, because it vividly underscores the value-perception pricing philosophy. In turn, waitstaff selling techniques must be critically examined and upgraded.

Side dishes are dish-up items that can be reconstituted or reheated to order from the steam table, pantry, or sauté line. They allow a customer to exchange a baked Idaho potato for garlic mashed potatoes, wild rice, al dente vegetables, or add an order of Creamed Corn Parmesan, Creamed Spinach with Anisette or any number of new interesting menu items.

Let's look at the profit potential of that Creamed Corn Parmesan. A #10 can of sweet corn with some cream and spices, a sprinkle of freshly grated Parmesan cheese, and 10 seconds in the cheese melter is all it takes. Bingo—a fabulous, flavorful new side dish, simply prepared, costing a mere 57¢ and worth a retail price of $1.95, or maybe even $2.50.

What operator would turn away from this idea?

Side dishes also permit a great promotional strategy to encourage patrons to share an item, a practice gaining favor in casual and fine-dining restaurants across the country. After all, we've done lots of sharing of Asian and other ethnic cuisines with never a second thought. In addition, side dishes have a minimal impact on the line set up. They are prepped in advance and feature a minimum of hands-on work.

In the '90s, the foodservice credo is "anything goes." The days of "no substitutions" are virtually gone. It's time to think of side dishes as a powerful marketing and merchandising tool able to inject fun, interest, diversity, and "wow" into your customers' menus, with a minimum investment in time, research, and development. This is the perfect opportunity for you to introduce some of your company's best lines of convenience foods, which can pass the quality test and become prime candidates for new and interesting side dishes.

STAND-ALONE DESSERT MENUS

I've always been amazed, even shocked, by operators who downplay desserts and fail to recognize them as the profit opportunity they are. The conventional wisdom is that desserts slow down table turns. While this might make some sense on a Saturday night at 7:30, what about the rest of the shifts when there is a minimal wait or no wait to be seated?

At a time when operators have to fight to keep their clientele, shouldn't they keep them in their establishment for as long as possible to continue applying sales and merchandising tactics? There's nothing more valuable in the foodservice business than to have seats filled with patrons.

There are five powerful reasons desserts should be a

number one consideration when showing your customers how to fine-tune the profit potential inherent in their menus:

1. Many of today's patrons are indulging themselves when they dine out. They may starve themselves for a week with low-calorie salads, chicken dishes, brown rice, and non-alcoholic beer. But when they visit your customers' establishments, they want to treat themselves well, and dessert leads the list of classic indulgences.

2. At a time when guests are critically evaluating the overall "dining experience," shouldn't operators want to suggest that patrons end the meal on an upbeat and "sweet" note? Desserts are often a restaurant's most appealing items, having the best flavor, color, texture, aroma, and presentation.

3. Desserts lead to coffee, tea, and after-dinner cordials. The gross profit on coffee or tea is usually in excess of 80%. After-dinner cordials like Courvoisier VSOP, Kahlua and Cream, or Bushmills' Irish Coffee often have gross profit contributions that exceed the profit made on the entrée itself!

4. Desserts showcase the chef's culinary skills or the restaurant's creative flair. Most desserts can be prepared by the kitchen using basic equipment and minimal effort, and offer a chance to be creative without much risk of failure. What's more, diners tend to remember desserts most; partly because they are served last, but also because they epitomize the "special occasion" feeling diners have about eating out, no matter where they choose to dine.

5. Dining out is a very social pastime. Whether a customer is enjoying a romantic evening out with a sweetheart, or Mom is avoiding cooking and the clean-up afterwards, going out to eat has become woven into the fabric of our society. Foodservice operators can promote that sense of togetherness, friendship, love, and good cheer by offering a menu item that isn't available at home, and one that can be shared by all. What could be nicer than a slice of hot blackberry pie á la mode, served with a couple of forks?

The dessert menu must be stand-alone. In other words, it should be completely separate from the main menu. Why include a dessert listing in the body of the regular menu—and then remove the menu after the appetizer and main course selections have been made? A waitstaff can practice advance selling of desserts, offering reminders such as, "Save room for the homemade pecan cheesecake." I favor the element of surprise that is achieved when the dessert menu arrives announced, and is then followed by the presentation of the dessert tray.

Dessert menus should be a different size than the regular menu. Preferably, it will be smaller—a single page with desserts on one side and after meal beverages on the other. Be sure to include coffee and specialty coffee drinks, teas, dessert wines, and liqueurs in the selection.

The design can be slightly different, while remaining consistent with the graphic image, logo, colors, and overall visual identity of the restaurant. The plastic jacket—or an equivalent that utilizes preprinted blank shells—offers the most attractive and economical presentation of dessert selections.

Dessert is the "special" moment in the meal, the grand finale of the dining experience. It's a good selling technique to create some drama around dessert, coupled with a bit of special "staging" that creates excitement and a heightened appetite. Dessert is an "impulse purchase" that can be easily triggered by suggestive selling. Encourage your customers to train their waitstaffs in the subtleties of impulse selling. Better yet, why don't you recommend a selling script, which guides the waiter or waitress in the presentation—to be made while clearing off the last of the main-course dishes. A sample script may be as follows:

> "I hope you saved a little room for dessert. Our crème brûlée is spectacular—maybe the best in the world! Would you like to try it?"

The waiter or waitress then pulls out the dessert menus and places them in the hands of the guests, and offers a brief encouragement to consider all the wonderful choices. After the guests have had time to survey the menu, the waiter or waitress should return with the dessert tray, tilted to showcase a dazzling selection of desserts. While rotating the tray, the waiter should describe in delicious detail all the selections offered.

As is usually the case, there will be those in the party who want dessert and those who will abstain. This is a great opportunity for the server as a salesperson. How do they sell a dessert to one or two people in the party without making the remaining people uncomfortable?

Recommend to your customers that they teach their waitstaffs to offer a couple of different desserts with two, three, or four forks, allowing everyone to have a "taste." This approach will stimulate interest, create a sense of adventure, and often leads to a second or third dessert sale. It works every time. It's the easiest way to break down the barriers to desserts by finding a way to sell just one or two—even if they're shared by an entire table.

Once you get on a dessert-selling roll, coffee, tea, cappuccino, espresso, and café au lait will soon follow. Once the first dessert is ordered, add-on sales seem to be easy. And what about the party of four that has said "no" to dessert? How about offering a complimentary dessert, not just as a "thank you," but as a carefully designed sampling exercise. Can you imagine a more powerful promotion program right there at tableside?

Selling desserts is both an art and a science. Operators need to commit to memory the following three steps:

1. Present a stand-alone dessert menu
2. Showcase the dessert tray
3. Follow up with after-dinner beverages

If this regimen is strictly adhered to by your customers, their incremental dessert sales can be substantial, and can generate as much as 2% of sales in new profitability. In addition, merchandising desserts is a process that is perfectly suited to a full range of convenience products. You, as the consultative seller, need only provide recipes and a little "promotional nudge." Recipes and marketing collateral, as you know, are everywhere, for every dessert imaginable. If you can successfully penetrate a customer's dessert menu by offering distinct promotion strategies, the main menu will be next.

DEVELOPING SIGNATURE APPETIZERS

Promoting special "signature" appetizers is relatively simple and easy to implement. It can produce immediate sales gains, hopefully for a new and imaginative food idea that you can supply.

The prime objective of a "signature" item is to create and design an appetizer that is perfect for sharing by the entire party at the table. It must be an item that has universal appeal, is unique to your customer's operation, and is unlikely to be prepared at home—in other words, a special treat—one that offers a totally unique taste or plate presentation. This is a natural "next generation" menu-engineering idea, which can follow the side dish and dessert menu promotions described above.

Common examples include pot stickers in a Chinese restaurant, special chips and homemade salsa in a Mexican restaurant, and bruschetta or focaccia in an Italian restaurant. The signature appetizer represents an item that can receive an automatic round of approval from all members of the dining party, and one that is ordered before the menus opened.

An item that is so wonderful, so delicious, and so connected with the spirit of sharing, can easily become an automatic order. Clearly, taking full advantage of these items listed in the appetizer section represents a real creative challenge. But it can be achieved with the help of a few pointers from you as a consultative salesperson.

- The merchandising of signature appetizers should be kept simple. Limit yourself to no more than two items on a table tent. Encourage your customer to invest in some creative design for his promotion piece, possibly using some marketing allowance dollars from a manufacturer. Use color and upbeat graphics to introduce the item. If possible, select a unique shape or design, such as a fancy oval, a cloudburst or an interesting border to draw the eye of the guest to the table tent. And probably most important of all, make sure the plastic table-tent holder is new, clean and shiny.

- Price points should be kept affordable. Set a selling price that is no more than 30-35% of the average selling price of the entrées on the menu. For example, if the average entrée price is $11, design the signature appetizers to sell at around $3.50.

- Prepare the signature appetizer in a large portion for a better presentation. Each dish should offer lots of food, be easy to eat, fun to share, and deliver a high degree of value perception.

- Teach the customer's waitstaff and bussers to place the signature appetizer's table tent in the middle of the table, directly in the line of sight of as many of the diners as possible. Make the guests pick it up to make room for their glass of wine or beverage. Never place the table tent to the side with the condiments.

- When guests are being seated, the host or hostess should, in a very low key manner, suggest a signature appetizer to share, while guests are deciding which entrée to select. By finishing this subtle, suggestive sell with an understated gesture to the table tent that features these signature appetizers, the host or hostess performs a very important selling function. This effective prompting can dramatically impact impulse sales, even before the food server or cocktail waitress arrives at the table.

- Suggest a sampling exercise to trigger a sale if the initial attempt does not stimulate interest. For example, let's say one of your customer's signature appetizers is deep-fried sweet potato chips served with a dipping sauce. Encourage them to have the kitchen prepare a sampler to offer to guests on a complimentary basis. No more than a taste, this approach adds fun and adventure to the dining experience, and will probably "nudge" at least one-third of the diners at a table to request a full order. A 15¢ investment in "food sampling" might yield dozens of $3.50 "signature appetizer" orders over the course of a shift.

The trends toward innovative side dishes, stand-alone dessert menus, and suggesting signature appetizers are based on a simple criteria—the importance of keeping entrée prices down, while simultaneously building check averages through aggressive tabletop merchandising and suggestive selling. To take advantage of these trends, but not overburden the operator's capabilities, DSR's should offer advice and counsel carefully, sparingly, and with full understanding of your customer's market image and reputation.

CHAPTER 15

BRANDING

A SLEEPING GIANT OF OPPORTUNITY

The suggestion of adding branded products to your customers' menus is the definition of "value-added" thinking and value-perception pricing. Brand identity is here to stay. Depending on the specific menu application, it can be extremely effective in increasing both the range and diversity of the food products offered. More importantly, the right branded products create instant credibility about product quality. Whether it's Grey Poupon Dijon mustard, Dreyer's/Edy's Grand ice cream, genuine Idaho potatoes, or Monfort's Chef's Exclusive steaks, the guest instantly recognizes the name of the product, and is predisposed to buying it.

An added benefit is that manufacturers carefully promote, protect, and advertise their brand locally and nationally. When showcased properly, these items can add to the operator's reputation for quality. Extensive research suggests that four out of five patrons believe a restaurant's image is enhanced by the use of branded products, and every food manufacturer has case studies supporting this hypothesis.

A perfect example of this dynamic is Prawns Sauté,— one of a restaurant's more popular dinner entrées. Originally selling for $15.50, Prawns Sauté can became Prawns Dijonnaise by simply adding 31¢ worth of Grey Poupon

Dijon mustard. The added value of the Grey Poupon allows a new selling price of $17.95, and can boost incremental sales by over 20%. Most importantly, the additional $2.45 is a decent return on 31¢ worth of mustard, wouldn't you say?

When the Dreyer's/Edy's Grand ice cream logo was added to the dessert section of another restaurant's menu, the operator added 50¢ to the selling price of each of these dessert items. Again dessert sales increased by over 20%. What did the guest subconsciously see? The full-color, 30-second TV spot the night before in which the Dreyer's/Edy's quality reputation was reinforced in glossy, vivid color. The flow-through profit increased, too, adding approximately 30¢ to each of these desserts sold.

How about genuine Idaho potatoes? In a successful steakhouse chain, the "genuine Idaho potatoes" logo was added next to a signature side dish—an add-on-sale potato sampler, featuring garlic mashed potatoes, cheddar potato skins, and Texas-cut fries. The food cost for this item was about $1.22. The brand name of the potato, and the logo featured on the menu allowed a selling price of $4.50. The guest perception is that they are getting the best quality potato in the world, served three different ways, satisfying their craving for a new flavor experience.

Branding must be done selectively and with caution. Menus should be accented by branded products, not driven by them. One or two percent of the items on a menu should feature a brand name or reference. Menu mentions and marketing allowances from the food manufacturer, can assist in promoting branded items. Rather than suggesting the use of an off-the-shelf table tent promoting a new signature appetizer of some kind, suggest that your customer use the allowances to develop original and exciting tabletop or menu images designed to introduce and spotlight a signature item.

Try to keep your customers focused on the tremendous

profit opportunities that branding can deliver. Think of the "profit leveraging" that can occur if, through intelligent and aggressive tabletop merchandising, you can use marketing funds to up-sell ten additional desserts per day, each sale providing an additional dollar of flow-through profit. That could mean $3,650 in new annual profit!

PART FIVE

THE FUTURE
AND
YOUR SUCCESS

CHAPTER 16

ARE YOUR CUSTOMERS AN ENDANGERED SPECIES?

After many discussions about the foodservice business with distributor salespeople, and sharing the various ideas, principles, and techniques that can be utilized in becoming a value-added "consultative seller," it's time to take a much-needed look at how my efforts, and those of others who offer progressive new ideas to distributors, have enabled DSR's to help their customers. How are salespeople doing in consulting with customers? Have they taught anything of real value? Have any of us actually helped operator customers?

I believe strongly that distributors who embrace and champion the kind of progressive thinking that is published in industry magazines, and discussed at foodservice seminars and meetings, will clearly see their revenues and profits soar. That has been my message during all my years as an industry educator and trainer. But, by and large, the information I've passed along to distributors and their salespeople has been tactical in nature. It consists of specific, usable, bits of information that you can draw upon as part of your selling regimen. Its main purpose has been to provide you with tools and insights that can help you gain credibility with your customer, and elevate you as a provider of value-added services.

Now I'd like to think and talk strategically. I'd like to share with you some observations about your operator customers and how they are meeting their guests' needs. Are the challenges of your customers changing in nature? How will they be handling these challenges by the year 2000? I'd also like to give you my view about where consultative selling is heading, and how it will become refined into a more useful, problem-solving, customer-responsive protocol.

I want to focus your attention on how to evolve into a better consultant by becoming a better diagnostician. The process begins by learning to be a better listener. Ask yourself, "How do I convert what I hear from my customers into a meaningful response that can really help solve their problems?" However, before you can start improving your listening and selling skills, it's valuable to examine the health of your primary customers and prospects: street operators.

THE "STREET OPERATOR"

The street operator represents the best sales prospect for DSR's. The proliferation of high-profile chains in highly concentrated suburban and urban commercial segments has emerged as a significant trend in most major markets. Self-distribution by companies such as Marriott Food Services, or Pizza Hut, Taco Bell, and KFC being served from one truck, supports the trend of chains across the country.

Clearly, the street operator is at the opposite end of the spectrum from the corporate chain establishment. And the heart of this street business is still the independent restaurateur. The progressive broadline distributor must see the independent street operator as a central marketing focus over the next five years.

A 1996 editorial piece addressed an important

question: "How will independent restaurants survive?" The writer quotes statistics from the National Restaurant Association, which found that the independent restaurant, while not thriving, is still holding its own in the face of chain domination. The editor's premise—and I think he is correct—is that the imagination and innovation of the independent, when coupled with the ability to re-concept almost overnight, will always provide a market advantage over the slow, cumbersome way in which most chains interpret market needs and guest preferences.

Yet despite the independents' tenacity in holding onto market share, consultant Victor Baker suggests that chains will continue to dominate the market. They can afford the best locations, provide serious marketing clout and brand-building awareness, offer better product consistency, cost management, and quality assurance.

I would venture to say that one or two percent of the market, independents whom we have identified as our primary growth vehicles, is replaced each year by well-managed chains with 21st-century marketing savvy. Boston Market, Kenny Rogers Roasters, and Chevy's are excellent examples of synchronized business machines that sell food in huge volumes at a quality level, until now matched only by the independent or street operators in their markets.

For broadline DSR's, this trend suggests a shrinking base of customers, and a matching increase in chains served by the self-distributing mega-giants. The immediate future portends a gradually shrinking universe of customers for the broadline distributor.

This brings the question of street business potential to front and center. It influences the development of marketing plans for every distributor who serves street operators. The reality of the marketplace, in my view, is that independent operators, despite their ability to innovate, to act and react to market forces quickly, and to go above and beyond the norm for guests, are losing the battle. Therefore, it is the primary mission of every DSR to address this with a "next generation" consultative selling approach, one with the aim of becoming the operator's true salvation.

In addition to becoming good listeners and good questioners, sales reps must refine their consulting discipline. The logical evolution of consulting is toward becoming a good "interpreter" of the operator customer's challenges. The DSR/consultant must develop the capacity for distilling and synthesizing data into action steps, then providing recommendations to their customers on the spot, responding quickly and efficiently to the smallest windows of opportunity.

Developing skill as a diagnostician is really another form of commitment to building long-term business relationships, and improving sales success. This type of business development, cultivated over time, requires patience and a willingness to adopt a different attitude about selling. It means nurturing your customers' most precious and carefully given gift: their trust. The DSR can build that sense of trust with his or her customers through the process of diagnostic selling: listening for the problem or the untapped opportunity, and then delivering information and resources quickly and effectively.

Diagnostic selling is the highest level of professional selling, producing maximum customer satisfaction and value perception, while driving higher distributor margins and DSR commissions. It epitomizes the "win-win" situation.

Usually, the diagnostic approach to consultative selling means helping shape and mold your customer's decision process, particularly relating to purchasing from you and your distributor company. If you have input into their decision-making process, you will be involved in your customers' introduction to and acceptance of new ideas, techniques, procedures, and disciplines. You will be the one to shepherd them through their preparation for and involvement in change.

How do you help facilitate the changes necessary in your customers' foodservice operations in a way that initiates purchasing decisions favorable to you and the products you represent? That is the most crucial questions for the foodservice diagnostician. In simple terms, you must separate the two actions of buying and changing. You must steer your customer toward buying from you as the desired outcome, and use the need to change as the event that gets you the customer's business.

Your customers buy for essentially positive reasons: to fulfill product needs, solve problems, improve quality, lower cost, attract patrons, and prevent loss. They want, expect, and need your advice and services.

Negative events, however, are unavoidable: food cost is too high; good line cooks are impossible to find; a new fryer is needed; the health department's recent inspection "punch list" is extensive; the precut steaks are lousy, and so on. These negative circumstances compel your customers to take action, to change. While it is never an easy process, with your help as a consultant, change can bring positive benefits.

In order to use change to your advantage, develop a five-part plan for every problem:

1. Clarify in excruciating detail what the problem is. What is causing the operator's pain, and where is it being felt?

2. Carefully guide your customer toward recognizing and accepting his or her part in the problem. Eliminate excuses.

3.   Quantify the problem. If you cannot attach a cost to it, then maybe there is no problem.

4.   Through discussion and good listening, convince your customer that you understand his or her problem.

5.   When appropriate, offer a solution in "reward-driven" terms. Quantify the anticipated results.

   For example, if you are suggesting that your customer eliminate the garbage cans in the kitchen for a month to better control food waste and lower food cost, you must present the solution as one that helps recover the $15,000 in lost profits. Always present your solutions in the form of annualized dollar savings.

   In the final analysis, it will be a partnership between the DSR and the independent operator that will save and preserve street business. For the DSR, it means moving to the next level as a diagnostician, helping the customer manage the decision process. In the absence of a structured involvement by the DSR, the decision process will always deteriorate to the lowest common denominator: price.

CHAPTER 17

THREE STEPS TO SUCCESS

I hope you never see or touch a menu in the same way again after reading this book. Menu analysis and awareness can work wonders and help you go a long way in building a successful consultative relationship with your customers. Plain old menus just don't pull their weight in a foodservice environment where marketing and promotion strategies can be so effective in building new sales and profits. Diners can be seduced and influenced by the well-designed and well-written menu. It's up to you, the knowledgeable DSR, to show your customers how to make it happen.

Value-perception pricing, when understood and applied, can put real dollars-and-cents success into your customers' operations through the manipulation of gross profit contributions. Help design your customers' menus as profit blueprints, and then provide some of the tools they'll need to transform these menus into a marketing plan. The DSR's task of developing "the profitability mind-set" may be difficult, but, to achieve any level of success, you must start now. Profitable consultations with customers is the direction in which foodservice distribution is heading.

I become energized when I think about the number of dollars in net profits that you, the profitability consultant, can create for your operator customers. I become even more enthusiastic when I think this can be done while simultaneously adding another 2% gross margin to the distributor end of the business. There are significant financial rewards for everyone: the food manufacturer, the distribution company, the sales reps, and the operator. There is also the satisfaction that comes from knowing that you've helped the foodservice industry deliver better products and services to the consumer.

So remember, your new life and mission as a foodservice DSR-turned-consultant is essentially a three-part commitment:

1. A specialized needs-assessment process, leading to a profile of your customers' problems, challenges, opportunities, and needs

2. An ongoing re-education process that teaches your customers about value-perception pricing and how it can deliver more advantageous gross profit contributions

3. The development of long-term relationships with customers by offering a consulting lifeline, which applies creative menu engineering, design techniques, and guest service disciplines to help them achieving higher sales and profits

This consultative approach will allow you to face the future with tremendous optimism. There is no longer a place in the foodservice-distribution business for DSR's who function solely as order takers. There is however a wide-open opportunity for consultative salespeople who are diagnostic thinkers who don't just sell products, they sell solutions.